"How Awesome Is This Place!"

(Genesis 28:17)

My Years at the Oakland Cathedral, 1967–1986

A Memoir

By

E. Donald Osuna

Aventine Press

Copyright © 2011, E. Donald Osuna
First Edition

Without limiting the rights under copyright reserved above, no part of this
publication may be reproduced, stored in or introduced into a
retrieval system, or transmitted, in any form or by any means
(electronic, mechanical, photocopying, recording, or otherwise),
without the prior written permission of both the copyright owner
and the publisher of this book.

Published by Aventine Press
750 State St. #319
San Diego CA, 92101
www.aventinepress.com

ISBN: 1-59330-730-6
Library of Congress Control Number: 2011907779
Library of Congress Cataloging-in-Publication Data
How Awesome Is This Place

Printed in the United States of America

ALL RIGHTS RESERVED

TO FLOYD L. BEGIN

First Bishop of Oakland and by Providence my first boss on the 50th Anniversary and Golden Jubilee of the church he proudly fathered.

with blessings
E D Osuna

ACKNOWLEDGMENTS

My heartfelt thanks to Mary Ellen Leary for editing the initial chapters and graciously guiding my literary efforts; to Jack Miffleton for his unfailing friendship, input and encouragement; to historian Jeffrey Burns for his scholarly review of the completed manuscript; and to Danuta Krantz for proofreading the manuscript and suggesting publishing options.

Most especially, I am grateful to photographer Jerry A. Rubino, whose work is featured throughout these pages. His faithful camera and artful eye has captured on film what many carry imprinted in our memory and engraved on our heart.

CONTENTS

PREFACE

WHERE IT HAPPENS

St. Francis de Sales parish became Oakland Cathedral when the new diocese, split from San Francisco, was established in 1962. The range of its ministry is exactly proper for a cathedral. It serves the local geographical community, folks from everywhere in the diocese, and welcomes guests from every part of the country and beyond. Every Sunday, the liturgical assembly is a picture of this diversity made one. The Church of Oakland is most especially alive in the liturgy of Oakland Cathedral, saved by the Word proclaimed among believers, nourished at the table of the Lord.

For more than ten years, Oakland has been a liturgical *Mecca* with a national reputation. It has been called vibrant, innovative, colorful, reverent, fun, exciting, prayerful, real and even "far out." It is not uncommon for "first time" participants, especially if they have been away from formal Church life for a while simply to weep as the experience unfolds. "The Church has changed," was the tearful admission of one young man, a self-styled prodigal, on a recent Sunday. The Greeting of Peace was more than he could bear! "These people really care for each other," he exclaimed.

What makes Oakland Cathedral a little different, in its own diocese and in the American Church? Vatican II started it all. As the Council ended, two young men began a program of liturgical renewal throughout the diocese in the effort to assist parish communities to have some *experience* of what the Constitution on the Sacred Liturgy invited. Newly ordained Father Don Osuna and Attorney-Musician John L. McDonnell, Jr. were convinced that a renewal would need more to ensure its success than simply an exchange or clarification of ideas. Ideas, of course, were crucial, but they didn't go far enough. People need to experience good liturgy if they were ever to be convinced of its power. And music was intrinsic, not incidental, to the experience. The Osuna-McDonnell program was ambitious. They contracted to spend six weeks of analysis and four more weeks of shared celebration with each parish they served. Ten weeks of therapy! Ten parishes and more than two years later, Don and John decided that there had to be a better way to organize and make available what they had to offer. They were convinced, of course, that their labors in any one parish could not be substituted for the work that the parish members themselves needed to do. While they could assist the experience of a community, they knew that it could not and should not depend on them.

So the decision was taken. Settle down in one community and expend full-time service there. Work for and with the members of the St. Francis de Sales community, so that community life and liturgy there would build up the Body of Christ in that parish. At the same time, structure programs of education and practice that would assist both parish members and representatives from through out the diocese. It was not only a splendid formula for ministry. It was exactly what a cathedral should do! At the heart of it, there was the overriding conviction that the most important and most persuasive element of all the programs that were undertaken was the celebration itself of the liturgy.

There is a stateliness and simple dignity to this otherwise undistinguished building in downtown Oakland. It sits across from the bus station, never a gathering place in any town for the performing arts, intellectual exchange or the principal social events of the community. There is a lot of stumbling misery up and down the streets that surround St. Francis and the neighborhood suggests that life has passed by, moved ten blocks or so to the banks and offices of a newer Oakland, forever charming in the romance of St. Francisco across the Bay. But the Cathedral is a place of life! The building is what a building should be: a place for people to gather. Robert Rambusch Associates uncluttered its interior and allowed the main lines of the space to become clear. This church is named for what is the definition of church: the community of believers.

Oakland Cathedral belongs to the community. In the final analysis, that is what makes it work. The people own what happens there. They design it, they execute it, they pick up the pieces afterwards (and reap the harvest as well!). The "parish community" includes both people who live within the geographical boundaries of St. Francis de Sales and others from the San Francisco Bay area who have committed themselves to membership. The combination makes for a splendid coming-together of ethnic, economic, educational and vocational riches. Indians, Filipinos and Hispanics pray and work with Anglos and Blacks. Students and professors of Berkeley's Graduate Theological Union and the Franciscan and Jesuit schools of theology, share ministry with blue collar workers and laborers. The retired elderly match the enthusiasm of teenagers.

"Task Forces" specify the distinct roles of ministry undertaken by community members who gather themselves in groups. They give their attention to youth, religious education, administration, spiritual growth, senior citizens and liturgy. Ned Barker, chairperson of the liturgy task force, has no doubt about what ties it all together: "liturgy forms the people, and the people shape the liturgy." Liturgy is the heart. He is not alone in this view. Liturgy is the center of everything that happens with the parish community. Everybody agrees on that! Artist Patricia Walsh, president of the parish council, affirms that at liturgy "the emphasis is on each other as the presence of God instead of on an abstract idea of God." From this weekly experience, she feels, everyone "is refreshed to go on, uplifted by what has been shared."

Nor does the liturgy trap the community into selfish preoccupation with internal concerns. The dynamism of their prayer always leads them *out*, to serve the world, so that what has been shared may bear its proper fruit. Concern for others is demonstrated very touchingly each Sunday when, at the end of communion, special ministers of Eucharist are sent forth with a simple but public mandate to feed incapacitated brothers and sisters and notify them of the community's continued affection and concern. Programs like last Lent's focus on the people of the Third World deliver the same message: we are all God's children and have responsibility for each other.

When the liturgy happens, it doesn't just happen! Careful and complex planning is the order of the day. The liturgy task force identifies the focus of each celebration by consulting the texts of the lectionary. Musical pieces are chosen because of (1) their harmony with the theme, (2) their quality, (3) their place in the celebration. Special activities, called for by the needs of a particular celebration, are assigned to the appropriate ministers. In addition to these somewhat routine matters, the special ingredient which must be counted as the major factor of influence is this: a liturgy, like every work of art, cannot be constructed by a committee. It must be fashioned by an artist. So, all the work of the liturgy task force, essential as it is, helpful as it is, ultimately is submitted to the creative hands and vision of one artist. At Oakland that artist is Don Osuna: musician, pastor, genius. No one begrudges Osuna that role, or envies it either. It is not regarded as authoritarian veto-power over the community but as artist's service for brothers and sisters. More than a decade of experience yields the irrefutable argument in favor of this arrangement: it works!

The pastor's role as chief artist hardly exempts the rest of the ministers from responsibility for their own tasks. John McDonnell, who directs the choir and ensemble, says that their musical style must be classified as "eclectic." A choir of forty-five voices, soloist Melissa Franek, and instruments (string bass/electric bass, two keyboards, two guitars, two trumpets, sax and flute, plus a string quartet for special occasions) conspire to make this gracious blend of styles into one "Oakland style." Ample use is made of classical, folk, jazz, swing, spirituals, soft rock, show tunes and even country western. The mix has developed over the years, shifting with the needs of the community and its characteristics.

An attempt by one young couple to summarize what happens at Oakland listed these points in this order: (1) people come, (2) who want to be part of it, (3) and find it comforting, (4) center all their life around the liturgy, and (5) insist on making it bear apostolic fruit. The first bishop of Oakland, Floyd Begin, somehow understood that Don Osuna had touched a central nerve. He was the galvanizing force that brought people together to pray and, if the bishop didn't come with great frequency himself, he made the whole thing possible for others. He made it possible for them to do it at his Cathedral, so that it wasn't long before it became clear that it wasn't "his" Cathedral at all but everyone's, including the bishop's. The present Ordinary, Bishop John Cummins, a native of Oakland, has made his own agreement with the Cathedral program all the more dramatic by moving his residence to the Cathedral rectory. "The Cathedral," he feels, "serves the community which makes up its parish, and serves the whole length and breadth of the diocese as well. A bishop today can't stay home. He needs to be everywhere with his people, to serve them." But one of the places to serve them is precisely at "home," at the Cathedral liturgy. The warm and affable Cummins is a welcome celebrant in the midst of the "home community." His homilies are especially appreciated.

Aren't there any problems at Oakland? Of course there are: the continual challenge to work with each other, to try over and over again truly to listen and to hear each other, taxes the patience of all. Over the years, particularly in an earlier age when traces of legalism were still in the air, more or less substantial shots were fired across the bow of Oakland's struggling ship. Occasionally a bomb landed, and shrapnel was made a permanent part of the bodies that were aboard. Once or twice, there was nearly a wreck, and some consider it "a real miracle that they are still together." Even success has been a problem, because it inspires people to foster inflated or misdirected expectations.

But in this age of liturgical renewal, when it is the mandate of the Second Vatican Council to develop forms of prayer which will be culturally appropriate to communities of men and women all over the world in all their diversity, it is still not possible to estimate the size of the debt that the American Church owes to the community of Oakland Cathedral. When the history of this time of reform is written, Oakland will hold a central place. Four words tell the reason: People, Prayer, Suffering, Fidelity. Several weeks ago, network television recorded the community liturgy of Oakland Cathedral for a national audience. May their film and these words provide some insight into the action of the Lord among His faithful people at Oakland, and serve to inspire us all!

John Gallen, S.J.

Hosanna: A Journal of Pastoral Liturgy, Volume 5, Number 2, 1979
Reprinted with permission by Oregon Catholic Press
5536 NE Hassalo, Portland, OR 97213-3638 liturgy@ocp.org

Prologue

On that momentous afternoon, the three of us were glued to the rectory television monitor. An American astronaut was stepping onto the moon and announcing a giant leap for mankind. Science and technology had wedded and were giving birth — right there in our living room — to a new age.

Just as memorable was Father Jim Keeley's comment at the end of the telecast: Gazing out the window at the silver sphere with an earthling now prancing about its surface, the young priest prophesied, "Wait until the poets get a hold of this!"

That was July 20, 1969.

Earlier in the decade, a similar landmark event had altered the course of church history. In 1962, the recently elected pope, like the visionary American president, had set his sights on a far-off target. President Kennedy took man to the Moon; Pope John XXIII brought the Catholic Church back to earth. For too long, the pontiff concluded, the bark of Peter had skirted the realm of human affairs like a satellite, detached, remote and locked into its own orbit. The ship had become obsolete; it was time for a return to earthly origins. Once grounded in its native soil, the Church could once again reclaim its pristine identity: that of a disciple and servant of the Lord Jesus Christ who alone had ascended into the heavens!

The trajectory was earthward; the propellant for reentry was to be the sacred liturgy. To achieve this, Pope John had convened the Second

Vatican Council which immediately engineered the reform of the Roman Rite, thereby taking aim, as one colleague put it, "for the jugular." Nothing is as sacred to the Church as its rituals which cradle and nurse so jealously its ancient creeds. At worship, believers experience what it means to be Catholic. For them, sacramental celebrations and especially Sunday Mass reveal and express the very essence of religion: the Word of God and Christian Tradition. So, in order to bring the Church around, the Pope and the bishops of the Second Vatican Council had to subject the sacred liturgy to review, revision and renewal.

The results were revolutionary. Out went the Latin, the ancient voice of a buried empire. Henceforth the sacred mysteries were to be proclaimed in the tongues of the people. Rubrics and ceremonials were restored to their original simplicity, eliminating centuries-old "accretions." Flexibility replaced the rigid and stylized rubrics of the Council of Trent (1545–63). Waves of changes and revisions began inundating beleaguered pastors.

Some critics claimed that the liturgical reforms reduced the sacramental structures to bloodless skeletons. But others considered it profoundly insightful of the Council to provide simple frameworks for local churches to adapt and enhance with local cultural and religious traditions. No doubt about it: Pope John, who was ready to embrace everyone he met, wanted the Roman Rite to be equally as catholic — welcoming, encompassing, incorporating into its worshiping embrace the diverse and distinctive heritages of the human family.

The pioneers had done the deed. Were there to be any poets?

*****

Floyd L. Begin, installed as the first Bishop of Oakland, attended every session of the Council and dutifully espoused the spirit and letter of its decrees. When the three-year conclave ended, he determined that his new diocese would be the first American see to implement its reforms. So the first thing the Cleveland native did upon returning from Rome was to hire Robert Rambusch of New York to refurbish his cathedral church. St. Francis de Sales was to be gutted and completely renovated to conform to the new liturgical norms — notwithstanding the history or sensibilities of the local parish community in Oakland, California.

The bishop's unilateral decision to reshape the diocese's mother church without local consent or consultation was bold, dramatic and provocative. But it was the quickest way to cast in concrete his commitment to implement the mandates of the Second Vatican Council. He too could aim for the jugular!

When it was dedicated on February 4, 1967, the gleaming edifice at the corner of Grove Street and San Pablo Avenue lit up the heart of Oakland's inner city. Ironically, it illuminated the gloom of the surrounding landscape: the dismal Greyhound bus depot across the street, the halfway house for convicted felons down the block, the decaying hotel and flophouses along the avenue. Its empty nave highlighted the equally forlorn and forsaken congregation: seniors from the surrounding high-rises and the residents of the low-income family dwellings nestled between apartment buildings and commercial storefronts. (The neighborhood had once been a prosperous enclave for Irish and Italian immigrants. But the war years had caused it to mutate into a haven for out-of-state job seekers and military-base personnel. The parish school, once an academy for the offspring of the original settlers, now tutored poor Hispanic children from the neighborhood and African-American youths from the nearby ghetto.) Why should these local folks attend the inauguration of a resplendent reconstruction that in their eyes represented a mausoleum commemorating the death of a treasured past?

If anyone had reason to be bitter, disgruntled and irate, it was Monsignor Richard "Pinkie" O'Donnell, pastor since 1942 of St. Francis de Sales parish and its first rector when Rome in 1962 selected it as the cathedral church of the newly created Diocese of Oakland.

"Let me tell you something, Father Osuna," he intoned shortly after I was assigned as his assistant, "I was serving Mass as an altar boy in this very church when the earthquake of nineteen hundred six shook this place to its foundation. The parish pulled through that tragedy just fine. But it will never survive what this bishop from Ohio has done to it. He didn't just gut the place, he has torn the heart out of the people!"

That was not all. Evidently, Bishop Begin had plundered the parish coffers as well. Rumor had it that in order to pay for most of the renovation, he expropriated all but $27,000 of the half million that the good monsignor had accumulated in savings over his twenty-five-year tenure!

O'Donnell was right. The "defacing" of the ancient shrine had completely demoralized the locals. There was a time, he pointed out, when they could point to the images of their ancestors who had posed as models for the host of saints that populated walls and ceilings. Now there was no one up there. All had been obliterated by a blanket of cream-colored paint! The transcendent stained-glass window of the Crucifixion above the high altar was gone, boarded over by layers of redwood paneling! The white marble altar, with its terraced columns and Gothic niches, had been dismantled and replaced by a bishop's throne! A masterpiece of renovation perfectly suited to the new liturgical norms? Perhaps, but to Pinkie and his people it represented an arid arena and a shameful sepulcher.

But events would soon prove Monsignor O'Donnell wrong. The people of St. Francis *would* recover. The arid arena would become a *Mecca* for pilgrims from the Bay Area and around the world. In time, thousands would flock to the Oakland Cathedral to experience the "creative liturgies" that began to enliven and rejuvenate the flagging inner-city parish. These vibrant weekly liturgies forged worshipers into a praying and caring community. Over time, the liturgies inspired and impelled them to reach out to others in Christian fellowship and social action. And it was to Sunday Eucharist that they returned each week to celebrate their identity and their work, and to be spiritually revitalized for the week ahead. In short, worship became the engine that sustained personal devotion and fostered expanded ministry, thus exemplifying the Council's definition of liturgy as "the source and summit of Christian spirituality." This memoir is the story of my life in that remarkable parish. As priest and artistic director, I spent nineteen years contributing to its creation and growing in its nurturing embrace. With countless others I experienced a vision, which, like that of Jacob at the shrine of Bethel, shaped my life forever.

When Jacob awoke from his sleep he exclaimed, "Truly, the Lord is in this spot, although I did not know it!" In solemn wonder he cried out: "How awesome is this place! This is none other than the house of God. This is the gateway to heaven!"
(Genesis 28:16.)

Original St. Francis de Sales interior, remodeled in 1967 (lower)

Seasonal liturgical design by Patricia Walsh

Prelude

Before It Happened

Theatre, music and art had been as much a part of my life as my desire to be a priest. As a boy soprano I sang solos from the choir loft at St. Louis Bertrand church in east Oakland. Monsignor Silva insisted that I become an altar boy and sent me untrained on to the sanctuary at the age of eight. Sister Kevin Marie, O.P., principal of the school, encouraged me to design artwork for the classroom and persuaded my mother to have me enrolled for piano lessons.

When I entered the seminary in Mexico City after the sixth grade, the rector recognized my musical potential and arranged for organ lessons. [Both my mother and father were from Mexico and agreed to have me study there, knowing that countless relatives would take good care of the youngest of their brood of ten children.]

After I transferred to St. Joseph's minor seminary in California, Father John Olivier, S.S., dean of studies and director of music, mentored me in the art of choral conducting and appointed me seminary choir director. Under his supportive wing I teamed up with Michael Kenny (the future bishop of Juneau, Alaska) to form K.O. Productions. Together we wrote original musicals (*California or Bust),* mounted and performed in Broadway plays (*Kismet, Harvey*) and tried our hand at Shakespearean theatre (*Henry IV, The Merchant of Venice*).

At St. Patrick's major seminary, where the focus was on the study of theology, the arts became strictly a personal pursuit. A group of fellow seminarians and I established the "Art Forum," where we encouraged each other to draw and paint, make stained-glass windows, delve into sculpture and even try our hand at bookbinding.

Always needing a musical outlet, I started a glee club. We performed classics such as Benjamin Britten's *A Ceremony of Carols* and *St. Nicolas Cantata* and gave concerts of American and international folk songs. I also was compelled to start a "gloom club" for those unfortunate souls who were unable to pass the audition for the glee club. (To my delight, some of these aspiring singers, like Dan Derry and Jimmy Tonna, actually learned to carry a tune!) Once a month I picked up my guitar and, along with a couple of my Mexican-American classmates, serenaded visiting families and friends with *musica ranchera*. These were satisfying enterprises that kept my creative juices flowing.

During summer breaks, I enrolled in undergraduate courses at Stanford University and Holy Names College in order to reinforce my natural musical and artistic skills with an academic foundation.

One would expect that, once ordained, a twenty-six-year-old priest would have no time for the arts. Not so, in my case. One year into my first assignment at St. Jarlath parish in Oakland, the order came to implement the reforms of the Second Vatican Council. This would involve revamping the sacred liturgy with its unique blend of all the arts — visual, musical, dramatic. Unlike some of my older colleagues, I was ready and well prepared — and eager — to tackle the challenge.

When the time came for "turning the altar around" in Advent of 1965, our pastor, Father Denis Kelly, took off for Ireland and left his three assistants to do the "turning." It was the beginning of an exciting and challenging task: designing a new altar, supervising its construction, and explaining to the congregation why the priest was facing them and saying Mass in English.

Things got even more exciting when Bishop Begin asked me to put together the music for the dedication of his newly remodeled cathedral. I composed and arranged much of the music, assembled and rehearsed a large choir and instrumental ensemble from parishes and local colleges, and got ready for the big event.

The ceremonies on February 4, 1967 were spectacular, especially the music that featured strings, harp, organ, flute, brass, chimes and tympani accompanying chorus and congregation. I remember the expression on my Irish pastor's face: He simply could not fathom how his young assistant had found the time and the resources to come up with such a jaw-dropping performance — with a harp no less!

The bishop was also impressed. A few months after the cathedral dedication, he appointed me Diocesan Director of Music and transferred me to St. Francis de Sales Cathedral as associate pastor with a mandate to create for the diocese a "model liturgy."

*****

In the summer of 1968, while I was on leave, Bishop Begin installed Father Michael Lucid, aged thirty-nine, as cathedral rector; he also assigned Father James Keeley, thirty-seven, as assistant pastor. Both were Irish-American, native San Franciscans and former high school teachers — credentials that appealed to the older clergy who were balking at the recent changes in the Church. But Lucid and Keeley were also students of history, keeping abreast of current events and very much in tune with the agenda of the Vatican Council. This delighted the progressives who were counting on the new team to bring from its storeroom "both the old with the new" (Matthew 13:52). No one would be disappointed. Even the seventy-five-year-old Monsignor O'Donnell would be charmed by the young churchmen who gently but resolutely took over the helm of his floundering parish.

Personally, my association with Mike and Jim was a turning point in my life. It made me reconsider my intended departure from the active ministry.

How had I come to that decision?

After six months in Pinkie O'Donnell's morbidly depressing rectory, I was on the verge of emotional collapse. The resentful monsignor refused to honor the bishop's mandate empowering me to take charge of the cathedral worship services. To that purpose I had previously contracted with my friend from seminary days, John L. McDonnell, Jr., to establish a cathedral choir. John was a probate lawyer and a musician whose forte and delight, along with the practice of law, was directing choirs.

I very much respected his musical talent and his taste for excellence. (I also enjoyed spending time with him, his brilliant wife, Loretta, and their three growing toddlers at their home on Trestle Glen.) I was sure that John's experience and my vision would result in a successful collaboration. Together, I felt certain, we could create a model liturgy for the diocese as the bishop had requested. The frustrated Monsignor O'Donnell, however, refused to provide the funds we needed to proceed, indignantly maintaining that all reserves had been "confiscated" by the Chancery.

Compounding the rectory situation was the general malaise that afflicted both Church and country in 1968. The U.S. had turned into a social battlefield: the assassinations of Robert Kennedy and Dr. Martin Luther King, Jr., the civil rights movement, the escalation of the Vietnam War, student uprisings and militant protests. Within the Catholic population a growing polarization over Vatican II reforms was exacerbated by Pope Paul VI's denunciation of all forms of artificial birth control in his famous encyclical *Humanae Vitae*. As a result, clergy, religious and laity became as unsettled as the beleaguered citizenry.

During those discouraging months, I found myself facing a personal question that had plagued me for a long time: Should I continue in a career that required one to be "all things to all men," or should I make use of my God-given talents and pursue the life of an artist and musician? Unable to resolve the conflict, I asked for a leave of absence and quietly left for New York City. There I spent a month with my brother Jess, a professional actor of stage and screen who had successfully mastered the realm of dramatic arts. Thanks to his hospitable and gracious mentoring, I feasted on an extravagant menu of cultural offerings until my artistic hunger had been sated and my soul satisfied. Revived, refreshed and reassured in spirit, I decided to quit the priesthood and pursue a career in music and the performing arts.

When I returned to Oakland, the only person I confided my secret to was my classmate and best friend, Father Tony Valdivia. Sheepishly I asked him to please call my parents and inform them of my decision. (I was too ashamed and afraid to do it myself.) This was more than he was prepared to deal with. Instead, he drove me to the Cathedral and declared, "There's a brand-new administration in place here. Give

Lucid and Keeley a try. If it doesn't work out after two weeks, I'll call your mother!"

Then he escorted me upstairs to my suite (the one next to Monsignor O'Donnell's). Once in my room, he began to unpack my personal belongings that were still in sealed boxes — lots of them. As each carton became empty he tossed it out the third-floor window onto the pavement below. That created quite a ruckus and roused the napping prelate next door.

Suddenly, there he was — Pinkie O'Donnell — standing in the threshold.

"Oh, it's only you, Osuna!" he roared. "For a minute there I thought we were having another earthquake!"

Chapter One:

Of Pioneers and Poets

Pinkie's sarcasm and personal animosity towards me were soon offset by my new boss's openness and no-nonsense attitude. Mike Lucid was not only broadminded and friendly — he was downright ecumenical. He even allowed me to get a dog — and a female at that! No doubt, he figured that a puppy would help the process of humanizing a household of celibates — which is exactly what Muffin did. One of the fondest images engraved forever in my memory is that of the four of us driving to a local restaurant for dinner on Tuesday evenings with Muffin comfortably enthroned on Pinkie's lap.

Despite the aged pastor's gradual mellowing, Pinkie continued to chide me. "What time does the circus start?" he asked me one Sunday morning as we passed on the stairway. A week later, however, I remember him remarking after one of our children's liturgies: "That was really nice!" Monsignor Richard O'Donnell died on May 23, 1971. His close friend and executor, Msgr. Charlie Hackel, asked me to perform at the funeral a selection he labeled as a "particularly appropriate anthem." The song's concluding lyric was: "The record shows I took the blows and did it *my way.*"

*****

Mike Lucid, our new boss, had a keen mind that sized up situations in a flash and an organizational skill that zeroed in on possible solutions. These gifts became evident at our first staff meeting.

"This parish has many needs and few resources. We will have to agree on a set of priorities. What do you think our most important undertaking should be?"

I suggested the parish school, because it was the only thing currently meeting an urgent need in the community. Moreover, the Sisters of the Holy Names who had staffed the school for eighty years were an influential and respected presence in the neighborhood.

"Education is important," Keeley concurred, "but I think that as a *church,* our *first* priority should be to teach our people to pray."

"Agreed," interjected Lucid. "Worship first, school second."

"Osuna," he continued, "you will take charge of all liturgical services, and Keeley will oversee all religious education programs. Now, I want both of you to report back to me next Tuesday on what strategies must be implemented and how much money will be needed to operate our targeted ministries. Agreed?"

Priorities, strategies, finances? This was sounding too good to be true! Was I really being invited to develop a liturgical program that would engage all my artistic interests? What a fabulous prospect: to use one's musical and artistic skills and adapt them to Catholic worship where all the arts naturally converge! The intended move to New York was off!

I immediately contacted John McDonnell and asked him how much he thought we needed to maintain an effective music program, including paid personnel and a large volunteer choir. "Five hundred dollars ($500) a month," was his response, adding, "that's the minimum!"

The following Tuesday, I gave my brief report: "In terms of strategy, I need to feel assured that I can spend as much time as needed on liturgical and artistic matters, and that when there is a conflict, others will cover the phones and doorbells."

"Agreed," Lucid confirmed. "Now, how much money do you need?"

"Five hundred dollars a month."

Lucid's face turned as white as the cathedral ceiling.

"Five hundred dollars? Do you realize that is one Sunday's collection — twenty-five percent of our monthly income?"

Keeley spoke up, uttering another one of his memorable sayings, "I believe that the definition of a priority is putting your money where your mouth is!"

"Agreed."

A few days later, Lucid asked to talk to me in private. "I understand that the diocesan music committee, of which you are the director, has arranged for the installation of a new pipe organ for the cathedral. I also understand that it will cost thirty-five thousand dollars. Is that right?" I nodded. "Well, the bishop has ordered me to pay for it out of our savings! However, there are only twenty-seven thousand dollars in that account. Furthermore, the school budget will require this year a parish subsidy of twenty-five thousand. I'm afraid that I have to ask you to postpone the purchase of the new organ."

Reluctantly I agreed, but I knew we were in deep trouble! Not having a pipe organ meant settling for an electronic (God forgive the concept!) replacement! There goes the quality of our music program! How can one properly accompany congregational and choral singing without the "king of instruments"?

Time to consult with John McDonnell again! The only way to ensure musical integrity, the wise attorney counseled, was to engage a permanent instrumental ensemble: strings, brass, piano ("At least that's an *authentic* keyboard!"), and additional musicians as the nature of the music required. It was a brilliant solution — and financially feasible. The addition of the live instruments would reinforce, legitimize and perhaps even drown out the sound of the "electronic bastard"!

As it turned out, the musicians we hired were mostly college music majors who were as proficient in popular musical idioms as they were in the classical repertory. (Among these extraordinary talents were Julie Meirstin on violin/piano and Bob Athayde on brass; the couple, who met at the cathedral, eventually married and are the parents of a trio of musicians, including Juliana Athayde, concertmaster of the Rochester Philharmonic Orchestra of New York.) As a result of such versatility, we chose music from a wide variety of styles. And because the people in the pews were from such disparate musical cultures, we programmed a blend of selections that at some point during the service would resonate in each praying soul, young and old, native and foreign, of whatever musical persuasion. Thus was born the "Oakland Cathedral Sound."

By 1971, even *Time Magazine* took notice:

> One church has discovered that a variety of music can attract worshipers. Nine years ago when it was designated the cathedral for the new Roman Catholic diocese of Oakland, Calif., the inner-city parish of St. Francis de Sales included little more than a commercial section of downtown. But one young curate, Father Don Osuna, has since been wisely encouraged to improve the liturgy. Now, twice each Sunday, the music runs the scale between such unlikely extremes as Gregorian chant and rock. On one recent Sunday, the mixture embraced both Bach's *Air for the G-String* and *Amazing Grace.* On another included a Haydn trio, Bob Dylan's *The Times They Are A-Changin'* and Luther's *A Mighty Fortress Is Our God.* Worshipers come from all over the Bay Area. The Sunday collection, once a mere $100, is now up to $800 a week. ("Troubadours for God," May 24, 1971)

Our eclectic approach was anything but haphazard or arbitrary. It was a result of lessons learned early on in our programming efforts and our determination to tailor the music to the cultural background of a multicultural group of worshipers.

When John McDonnell and I put together our first Sunday liturgy for the sparse, reticent and what we considered "old church" congregation, we selected all traditional hymns, with the exception of one contemporary religious "folk song" by Joe Wise, "Take Our Bread." It called for a guitar, which in those days was considered a strictly secular instrument and unsuitable in church. To render the piece more palatable we had the keyboards and strings play along with the guitar. To our surprise, the people loved it. The simplicity of the melody and the quaint sonority of the guitar had an instant appeal that complemented the traditional hymns. It sounded "right."

This prompted us to take a closer look at the divergent tastes of our people and find music that reflected and reinforced their cultural sensibilities. In time, we began introducing other musical idioms such as Negro spirituals, gospel selections and hymns in Spanish to reflect the diverse ethnic makeup of the growing congregation. The inclusive nature of the musical menu set the crowd at ease and bolstered an ever stronger active participation.

The secret of success, we discovered, lay in programming the various musical styles in a logical and appropriate sequence. Every liturgy, for example, began with a classical prelude performed by the full choir and ensemble, e.g. Bach's "Jesu, Joy of Man's Desiring," a polyphonic motet or a setting by a modern composer. The entrance song would be a traditional congregational hymn accompanied by keyboards and brass: "O God of Loveliness," "How Great Thou Art." This combination created a palpable connection to the past and provided a feeling of security and comfort. In contrast, the recessional would generally feature a modern hymn or a rousing Gospel anthem: "Pass It On," "Ain't Got Time to Die." This prepared the rejuvenated worshipers to confront with resolve the world they were about to reenter. Within the Mass itself, we programmed contemporary compositions from the library of popular and religious folk songs: "Psalm 42: As the Deer Longs," "The Prayer of St. Francis." The entire ensemble reinforced the natural ebb and flow of the liturgy with its inner dynamic of climaxes (the Gospel Acclamation, the Great Amen, and Communion Song) and meditative movements (after the First Reading and following the Communion Song).

I was convinced that this kind of stylistic blending reflected the cultural psyche of the typical American audience, which seems to be more at home with a musical amalgam than a sustained dose of a single type of music. It is a phenomenon that every successful variety show producer knows so well. Virtually every television spectacular and special presentation invariably features a well-packaged mix of opera and the classics, Broadway musicals, popular, jazz and any other repertory that will appeal to the consumers whom the sponsors intend to capture. And so, artistic directors typically put together a "product" containing something for everyone. This is the American way. It works. It was only logical for an American liturgist to baptize it. After all, the people who watch *Saturday Night Special* are the same souls sitting in our pews on Sunday morning.

The Vatican Council's document on the sacred liturgy confirms this view. It states that in ministering to the faithful, "pastors must promote liturgical participation taking into account their age and condition, their way of life, and standard of religious culture." This norm was dubbed the "pastoral principle." The U.S. Bishops' Committee on the Liturgy defined it as the judgment that must be made in a particular situation and in concrete circumstances. "Does music in the celebration enable these people to express their faith, in this place, in this age, in this culture?" (*Music in Catholic Worship*, #39). As liturgists and musicians, we at the Oakland Cathedral adapted this pastoral principle to the profile of our people.

Our music program, however, was always at the service of the Word of God — the two were inseparably wedded. The music announced, reinforced and recalled throughout the celebration the biblical theme contained in the readings of the day. At the beginning of the liturgy, for example, the prelude and entrance song introduced the theme to be proclaimed in the Scriptures and elaborated upon later by the homilist. The Offertory Song immediately following the sermon served as a commentary upon or a response to the entire Liturgy of the Word. And finally the Communion and Closing Songs echoed the gospel theme as the worshipers shared the Body and Blood of Christ and took the Word with them into their homes, offices, schools and marketplaces.

My friend Father Tony Valdivia, always the insightful critic, once put it this way: "Your selection of music is a homily in itself."

*****

The "eclectics" are a very "catholic" phenomenon borrowing tastefully from a variety of sources and blending the selections in a patchwork effect which is aesthetically pleasing and rewarding. Campus worship particularly reflects this kind of approach and the fine choir and ensemble at the Oakland Cathedral is its epitome.
Ken Meltz, "Musical Models for the Eighties," *Pastoral Music* (April–May 1984)

Don Osuna and members of the Cathedral Ensemble

John L. McDonnell, Jr. conducting the Cathedral Choir

Chapter Two:

We Hold a Strange Hope

By the summer of 1969, the crowds at the 10:30 a.m. and 12:15 p.m. Masses had significantly increased as more Catholics and curious pilgrims from around the Bay Area discovered the Oakland Cathedral. They were an eclectic lot: simple folk from the inner city, visitors from other parishes, academics from neighboring colleges and a smattering of tourists from around the world. Many were drawn by the extraordinary music program; others came out of curiosity to see what fresh twist the Gospel would receive in the "creative celebrations."

Along with music, we blended the visual and dramatic arts to underscore and enhance the Liturgy of the Word. One of our earliest efforts was a four-week series commemorating the end of an era. *We Hold a Strange Hope* became the focus of meditation for the Advent liturgies in the final days of the historically devastating decade of the 1960s. Our goal was to look at the events convulsing the world, the Church and the country from the perspective of the Gospel, which, as the word implies, contains "good news." Hopefully we could provide a positive spin to a negative issue. How strange is that!

The curious were not disappointed this first Sunday of December 1969.

There, encircling the granite altar of the tastefully remodeled Norman-Gothic sanctuary, loomed the blown-up portraits of Che Guevara, Joan Baez, the Reverend Martin Luther King, Jr. and Neil Armstrong

The young Chicano homilist (Father Tony Valdivia) assigned to answer the question "Hope in Today's World?" was reviewing the shattering events that had obliterated the composure of the planet in a matter of seven years. It was a litany of crises in a decade of despair: "Cuba, Dallas, Selma, Atlanta, Watts, Kent Sate, Berkeley (not ten miles away), the Black Panthers (headquartered across the street!), Vietnam — and now Nixon!"

The preacher's insightful commentary did not prophesy an approaching doomsday. Rather, basing his analysis and assessment of the times on the promises of Scripture and the lessons of history, he called for a renewed confidence in God's power to redeem, and the Human Family's ability to transcend any obstacle. "After all," he concluded, pointing to the central photo above the altar, "have we not, at the end of this very decade, reached for and landed on the Moon?"

On the following Sunday, the same congregation returned to find, staring at them from the sanctuary, the image of one solitary revolutionary: the smiling face of Pope John XXIII. The topic: "Hope in the Church?" This time the preacher was Monsignor Frank Maurovich, editor of the diocesan weekly, *The Catholic Voice*. The clever journalist was pretending to interview the Pontiff who eight years before had summoned the Second Vatican Council with the simplicity of a child lighting a match in a dynamite factory.

The initial question addressed to the papal icon unfolded into a string of desperate charges: "How can Your Holiness justify the shambles in which you have left the Church? Was it your intention to open the windows so that all of our priests and nuns could scramble out, along with our youth and the older folk who can no longer recognize their own religion? And what about *Humanae Vitae*, the latest encyclical by your handpicked successor: Is that also part of the conspiracy to further encourage this mass exodus? Where will it end, Pope John, where will it end?"

"Well, Monsignor," came the response from the presiding portrait (the homilist had turned ventriloquist), "let me ask *you* a few questions: Are you concluding that because many have left the Church they have by that fact abandoned their faith? Are you suggesting that in exposing the deficiencies of our present tradition, we are indicting the Gospels? Have you forgotten the seminary axiom: *Ecclesia semper reformanda* (the Church is to be constantly reformed)? Would you have counseled

Christ not to have convoked the gathering at Calvary on the grounds that many would flee the scene? Did you think that the revolution shaking the foundations of every institution in the world would leave the Catholic Church untouched? Tell me, my dear Monsignor, am I the only one who still holds a 'strange hope'?"

No, he wasn't the only one. People everywhere were sincerely hoping to find spiritual bonding with God and one another. "Community" was the prevailing imperative of the times. John XXIII and John Kennedy had provided the world with the briefest vision of "Camelot" and of "The City of God" where peoples could be welded together in pursuit of the highest ideals. More recently, an idealistic and youthful generation was searching for mutuality and support at "Woodstocks" and in rural "communes."

And we at the Oakland Cathedral were making a concerted effort to create community through meaningful, vibrant and prayerful worship. It was working. The liturgies were attractive and engaging. Local parishioners were drawn back into the "arena." Wounds started to heal as the alienated discovered the welcoming and stimulating communal experiences. In short, we were becoming the "family" of St. Francis de Sales. As "mother church" of the diocese, we were also learning how to graciously embrace the growing crowds of community seekers from throughout the area.

The one who was responsible for introducing additional art forms such as dance and audio/visuals into our liturgies was Father Jim Keeley, our enthusiastic and indefatigable associate pastor who spent much of his time with the teachers and kids at the parish school. His lively presence and constant "God love ya!" reverberated throughout the halls and classrooms, inspiring faculty and students to work hard, have fun and dream great dreams.

Father Jim was as hardworking and fun-loving as they come. And his great dream was to reconnect the school with the parish. (Over time the two populations had drifted apart and rarely related to each other.) He put forward an ingenious proposal: "Let's involve our school kids in the parish's liturgy on Sundays." Summertime would be ideal, he noted, because the children could be prepared and trained during the forthcoming Summer School Project, which was to last five weeks. "After the final Mass," he suggested, "we can put on a 'Cathedral

Carnival' as a fund-raiser for the school!" He even proposed a theme for the first July Summer Series. We should call it *Life, I Love You!* (an English translation of the recurring Greek phrase in one of Lord Byron's poems, *Zoe mou sas agapo*).

The faculty and staff were eager to begin, Father Keeley announced. "All we need is for Father Don to pull it all together!" This would be a challenge. Working with children had never been my forte. I did have, however, some experience directing children's choirs and coaching youngsters in dramatic skits. I would have to find a way of including children as key ministerial elements into a medium designed for adults. It was worth a try. Besides, I felt that the entire enterprise was a stroke of genius!

The concept of a ritualized children's liturgy was virtually unknown in those days. There were no official guidelines or regulations. One had to proceed solely on instinct and the general ground rules set forth in the documents of Vatican II, which essentially said: *Get everyone, young and old, to internalize and express their faith by actively participating in the Church's worship.*

Actually the challenge was a winning proposition from the start. We soon discovered that children, when performing for an adult audience, can get away with just about anything. In our case, we found that our well-rehearsed and tutored kids became a catalyst transforming cold and isolated churchgoers into a warm, open-hearted community. Experiencing the children at prayer reminded one of the mystery of human innocence, underscoring the relevance of Christ's admonition: "Unless you become like little children, you will not enter the kingdom of God."

The process of preparing for these Sunday Masses uncovered hidden talents among the children and taught them new skills. Through ensemble singing, dancing and the art of dramatic presentation, they learned the rudiments of artistic discipline. By sewing costumes and creating liturgical art pieces, they learned to incarnate spiritual realities in images and sacred icons. Each day, the children were reminded that the sole purpose of their artistic efforts was to help people pray and worship God in a more vibrant and prayerful way. Weekly rehearsals in church introduced the children to the special magic of God's house — a sacred place where people came together to encounter their Heavenly Father.

One of the highlights of the series — along with the children's choir, of course — was the disarming little *corps de ballet* that our own dancing nun, Holy Names Sister Mary Gene Heller, had trained as a "movement choir." As a veteran educator, she knew that children naturally expressed their feelings through body gestures. Why not their faith? As the Offertory Hymn was being sung, the brightly costumed youngsters interpreted the sacred lyrics with graceful arm and body movements.

But the *piece de resistance* was a slide presentation, which was projected onto a movie screen located in the cathedral sanctuary. Steve Essig, one of our instructors and a gifted photographer, created a tapestry of snapshots. In projected transparencies it depicted our delighted school kids at home, at school and at play, enjoying as only children can, the simple pleasures of their inner-city surroundings — and having the time of their lives! The visual montage amounted to a commentary on the poet's ode "Life, I Love You," but also on Jesus' words: "I have come that you may have life, and have it to the full." Never had the Gospel message been proclaimed with greater impact.

As novice liturgists we learned two important lessons from these early experiments. One was that children, when properly coached and motivated, can be extremely effective ministers of the Word. They can capture a congregation's imagination, open up hearts, and even broaden the minds of the most skeptical. For example, the fact that a makeshift movie screen was obstructing the view of the altar no longer mattered; the images and the charm of those children had transformed the screen into a pulpit.

Secondly, we realized that the liturgy in English possessed a power to touch and move people's souls as never before. What had been lost by the suppression of the stylized liturgy in Latin could be replaced and even enhanced by an artistic and prayerful use of traditional and contemporary art forms.

Moreover, the musical and visual arts, which were undergoing such technological advances, could surely be adapted to the requirements of the liturgical reforms. New "hardware" was available that could be tailored to the service of contemporary churchgoers and their worship. In other words, the Gospel could be as freshly addressed in church as it was on the Broadway stage. Jesus Christ, after all, is the "Superstar" of every Eucharist.

St. Francis de Sales School children's choir

Jack Miffleton preaching at a children's liturgy

Chapter Three:

Reaching Out

It wasn't long before Lucid announced that we were ready to adopt a third priority. "With attendance on the rise," he explained, "the Sunday collection has doubled. We can continue," he said, winking at Keeley, "to put more money where our mouth is." He then suggested we concentrate on ministering to the very large population of older folk who were living in the surrounding high-rises. "We should establish a ministry to the elderly," he proposed, "and we should hire Holy Names Sister Thomasine McMahon as coordinator. Good?"

"Agreed."

This is how the legendary Sister "Bear" McMahon (a nickname shared with her priest-brother Tom, both of them being noted for their fierce commitment to social justice issues) arrived at St. Francis de Sales Cathedral. Sister Thomasine at once became a fixture on the streets and in the senior centers of downtown Oakland. Immediately, the feisty and no-nonsense nun organized a Thanksgiving Day meal for the down-and-out of the central city — the first of a yearly event that in time grew to include a clientele of over eight hundred homeless and hungry souls.

Her main mission, however, was to invade senior residences and convalescent homes and arrange for the elderly guests and patients to obtain the basic physical and spiritual necessities of life. To this end, she not only procured the services of lay volunteers but also persuaded reluctant government agencies to supply needed assistance — or else!

One of the most significant traditions she originated was arranging for lay people to take Holy Communion to the sick and shut-ins of the area. To do this, however, she had to get around the prohibition for anyone but a priest or nun to touch the sacred Host. We came up with an ingenious strategy to get around the matter. A solemn "commissioning ceremony" was introduced at the end of every 10:30 Mass. The volunteer "ministers" would be called forward and presented with gold containers with the consecrated Hosts. The celebrant would then officially depute them in the name of the priests and people of St. Francis "to go to the homes of our brothers and sisters who cannot join us around this table and assure them of our love, support and union in Christ." (Today, this is standard practice, and a good example of the restoration of an ancient custom.)

> After communion at the main Sunday mass, about 75 people stand in the sanctuary each with a host or two in her or his hand. The presiding priest, following the final prayer, commissions them with a charge that goes something like this: *You special ministers of mercy to the sick, go now and bring the Lord to our beloved parishioners confined within nursing homes, at hospitals and their own houses. Tell them this is today's message* (he summarizes the homily in a sentence or two). *Tell them they are in our prayers. Tell them we need their prayers, their sufferings, their lives.* He blesses the ministers and the congregation. Then the cross and candle bearers lead the recession out of the cathedral, followed by the 75 ministers. That action, repeated week after week, teaches in a powerful way how the entire Christian communion present and absent forms one body in the Lord. ("A Creative Worship Service," *Celebration*, June 30, 1985)

Sister Thomasine's foray into the neighboring community was matched by Monsignor Lucid's equally successful ecumenical overture to our Protestant brethren. He struck up a happy friendship with the Reverend Boyce Von Osdel, the exuberant pastor of the First Baptist Church of Oakland, located a short block away. Their mutual fondness blossomed into an enriching and long-lasting relationship between our two churches. The like-minded churchmen began by collaborating on inner-city projects and ended up by sharing theological profundities over lunch. One day, Lucid suggested that in keeping with Vatican II's emphasis on ecumenism, they bring their two congregations together for a joint worship service.

"Agreed!"

The Baptists offered to host the first reunion. Monsignor Lucid, accompanied by Keeley and myself, led a large contingent from St. Francis de Sales on foot down 22nd Street to the beautiful stone structure at the corner of 21st Street and Telegraph Avenue. Once inside, he gingerly mounted the First Baptist Church's pulpit. He prefaced his sermon with these memorable words: "Brothers and sisters in Christ, we Catholics traveled one short block to join you today in worship. My only regret is that it took us four hundred years!"

Thereafter, joint services were celebrated twice a year: in January during the Week of Prayer for Christian Unity and on Reformation Sunday in October. The relationship with our Baptist "cousins" grew stronger and deeper over the years. Joint religious education and Bible study programs and numerous social projects reinforced and confirmed our respect and genuine esteem for one other.

The unusual partnering was not lost on the national Baptist scene. The following article appeared in *The American Baptist*, July–August, 1978:

Catholic-Baptist Dialog Aids Fellowship in Oakland

OAKLAND, ca ---The late Pope John XXIII opened windows which for too long had been closed to meaningful dialog and fellowship between Roman Catholics and other Christian communities. In Oakland, CA, two churches, St. Francis de Sales and the First Baptist Church, are addressing each other through those windows and sharing a common challenge to ministry.

"Our feeling was that the job of redeeming the inner city of down-town Oakland is too big for anyone," recalled Dr. Boyce Van Osdel, pastor of first Baptist.

Inspired by the prevailing spirit of openness in 1970 the two churches established cooperative programs, and encouraged dialog, growth and closer relationships between the congregants.

Programs for senior citizens and youth, candidate forums in pre-election times, dinners and religious education for preschoolers, along with ecumenical worship services suggest that grassroots ecumenism is taking hold.

A Lenten series brought together members of two congregations to discuss the Eucharist, baptism, "marriage and orders," with the clergy presenting opening statements.

"What impressed me was our nearness," Van Osdel observed. "We were so close. What separated us was really not theology, but church politics, organization and structure — the way of doing things."

Van Osdel discovered that the two bodies "had pretty much the same outlook with reference to the Lord's Supper and baptism, even though we have different modes."

The Catholic Voice, Oakland diocese's newspaper, carrying news of the joint venture in faith, quoted Van Osdel: "As one has two hands to do a task, you might say downtown Oakland has two hands."

What characterized both Sister Thomasine's and Monsignor Lucid's outreach programs was their connection to liturgy. Both found not only that liturgical celebrations inspired them to go forth with outstretched hand in service and friendship, but that they were capable of embracing and welcoming those with whom they had established new bonds. Worship became an intrinsic element and impetus of outreach.

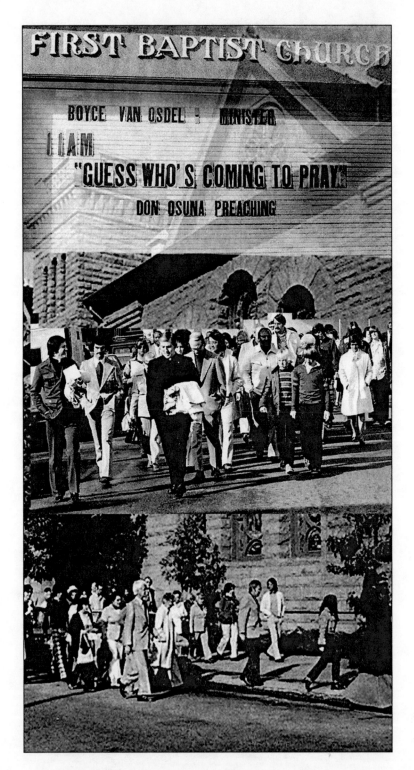

Pilgrimage to ecumenical service at First Baptist Church

Pastor Boyce Van Osdel (upper right) welcoming Catholic guests

Chapter Four:

Faces in the Revolution

Realizing that worship could foster additional relationships with the "outside world," Jim Keeley and I set out to design a second summer series that would do just that. As it happened, Lucid informed us that he would not be around to participate in the summer events; he would be in the State of Washington pursuing a Master's Degree in Religious Education.

"I'm sure that you and Keeley will keep everything under control," he commented upon his departure.

"Of course," we replied. "Don't worry about a thing, we're just going to keep on reaching out, like you, to the people around town!"

Jim Keeley and I had agreed that we should explore the so-called "revolution" and its instigators mentioned during the previous Advent. Once identified, we could invite some of them to share their perspective and objectives with our congregation. Together we could examine and celebrate the gospel dimension of their contributions. We christened the series "Faces in the Revolution."

The first group of "revolutionaries" we sought out were the farm workers of Delano in California's central valley whose dynamic leader and spiritual guru was Cesar Chavez, a devout Roman Catholic. Anyone who went to a grocery store at that time knew about the grape boycott that had been mounted throughout the country. And anyone who frequented Safeway supermarkets would probably have been confronted by demonstrators and sidewalk pickets. So, most churchgoers had a firsthand knowledge of the group of Hispanic "upstarts" whose faces and fate were flashed upon the giant screen in the Cathedral sanctuary that first Sunday in July 1970.

John Lodato, a parishioner and freelance photographer, volunteered to live for a while among the farm workers in Delano and try to capture on film the inner spirit of these migrant workers in revolt. His remarkable photo closeups revealed the bitter hardships the laborers and their families were enduring, their unshakable determination to prevail, and the deep religious devotion that permeated their resolve.

The photos were made into transparencies and assembled into a slide presentation that far surpassed our initial makeshift piece on the schoolchildren. Since then, we had consulted with technicians from Kodak who designed for the cathedral sanctuary a state-of-the-art rear-projection system with special carousels and lenses that projected the images onto a giant screen behind the main altar. The end result was an imposing "stained glass window" that reflected a sacred story with an ever-changing stream of images.

Scripture and special music accompanied the visuals, providing an added spiritual and biblical dimension to the farm workers' basic human quest. The impressive result was a contemporary commentary on the Beatitudes. Paraded before our eyes marched the "poor in spirit" of our day, the "meek," the "hungering and thirsting for justice" — the "blessed" of our times. When the presentation was over, everyone, enlightened and moved, joined in fervent prayer for these brave and heroic crusaders from the fields of California: May they one day soon inherit the earth!

*****

The second group of "social disturbers" who were invited to show their faces at our Summer Series lived just a few blocks away in downtown Oakland: the hardcore drug addicts-in-rehabilitation of Synanon.

Synanon was the original addict-oriented live-in therapeutic community where drug abusers came together for mutual support and voluntarily submitted to a strict regime of "continual confession and catharsis." Soon after arriving at the Cathedral, I had been invited to visit the facility. I became friends with several talented musicians in rehab, including a gifted composer and a professional vocal coach/ choral conductor. They got very excited about the prospect of creating an original cantata to be performed in the local Catholic cathedral. As one might imagine, the idea of inviting a group of recovering addicts to proclaim the liturgy of the Word was unprecedented and, in its own way, "revolutionary."

Unlike the photographed farm workers, the "blessed" contingent from Synanon appeared in the flesh. Their forte was music — and did they fill the cathedral rafters with sound! A large jazz band, augmented by an amplified rock group, and a forty-voice stable of singers belted out a cantata of joy and hope so profound that it reverberated through the inner chambers of every enraptured worshiper. So vibrant and fresh was the presence of those chanting warriors that one could feel the strength and courage of a David before his menacing Goliath. The sheer verve and conviction of their song suggested that a mighty foe could be defeated by the simplest of weapons.

It was ironic that people who would have been repelled the day before by these recovering addicts were that day being transported by them into religious ecstasy! I can still remember the tardy eighty-year-old parishioner, strolling nonchalantly to her regular pew across from the choir, fingering her rosary beads in the midst of a maelstrom of wailing saxophones!

Needless to say, that liturgy convinced us all that the revolution these folks were engaged in — the effort to turn their lives around — was cause for celebration and support. From that day on, our neighbors at Synanon became welcomed members of the Cathedral family.

The final "Face in the Revolution" was that of the Clown.

We had been persuaded by a recently ordained Jesuit who frequented our liturgies while a student in Berkeley that the exemplar of all radicals and rebels was Jesus Christ. And the image that most accurately portrayed what he accomplished, he maintained, was that of the Clown. "He twists things around and upside down, not to destroy nor for gain, but simply for love of life." "Jesus, the preeminent Clown," stated this son of St. Ignatius, "does the greatest balancing act of all time — right there on the Cross! . . . Some Fool!"

Father Nick Weber, S.J. was a clown himself — a professional one. His Jesuit superiors had granted his request to undertake a unique ministry: to gather together a troupe of trained performers and a few animals, and form the "Quarter Ring Liechtenstein Circus." It would travel around the country spreading the Gospel at college campuses and public parking lots.

We invited Father Nick to bring his circus into the Oakland Cathedral for the last Sunday of July 1970. What happened next became a *cause celebre.*

I remember feeling a growing sense of panic at the dress rehearsal the day before the performance as the circus performers set up their props, converting the area at the entrance of the Cathedral into a "quarter ring" circus arena. (At the same time, I noticed that the children from the summer school who were also to perform at the Mass the next day behaved as if something magical was about to happen.)

First of all, Father Nick announced that he would be "eating fire" as we processed into church, and mentioned something about how a "sidekick" would be handing him the torches. He was subsequently persuaded to reschedule that ritual for the recessional on the way out — when the congregation might be a "bit more receptive."

Then came the preview of the homily. Nick announced that the sermon he had prepared would be delivered by his associate — in mime. It was to be a "parable without words." All of us were caught completely off guard by what came next! Remember, this was 1970, at the height of the Vietnam War!

Out comes this young man in white-face, prancing about the sanctuary like a little boy playing with his toys. All of a sudden he discovers a toy gun. Gleefully he loads it, points it at imaginary enemies, and begins shooting. What fun!

Abruptly the child becomes a young man who is being recruited into the military. Now he is a real soldier and is issued a real weapon that he is being trained to use — for real. Seconds later he's on a boat being shipped overseas — to a real war. An order is given and off he marches into the battlefield. Bombs all around — gunfire; then he sees the enemy on the attack right in front of him! As trained, he slowly picks up his real rifle, puts it to his shoulder, takes aim, and fires!

Everyone can "see" the victim falling to the ground, shot dead by our carefree youth turned unwitting assassin.

The most excruciating expression comes over the mime's face as he realizes that he has actually killed a real live human being. In an exquisite pantomime of grief, he makes his way to where his victim lay and, with heartrending compunction and remorse, picks up the corpse, cradles it in his arms, slings it over his shoulder and hobbles off into the darkened sacristy — in dead silence!

There is dead silence as well in the pews.

I turned to Father Nick and asked incredulously, "Is this the Circus? Is this love of life? Do you realize what effect this piece is going to have on the congregation? We'll never be able to recover from the impact of the message! This is an indictment of the American people's role in the war!"

"Oh, do you really think it's that strong?" he asked.

"Look," I said, "it's perfectly OK to point out our sins, but we have an obligation as ministers of the gospel to proclaim a way of redemption as well."

"Well, I thought I did," he retorted. "The soldier, who represents us all, realizes that he just shot someone who he was taught was his enemy but was really his brother. So he wades through the hostility, embraces his victim and carries him away. Maybe he was able to revive him . . . or even himself."

Father Nick was right, of course. But how to break the paralyzing spell that the homilist was sure to cast over the congregation? And what would help them recover from the shock?

We took a break and pondered the situation.

"I have it!" I exclaimed in a flash of inspiration. The answer was right in front of us. "The children!"

I summoned the students around the organ console. "Kids," I asked, "do you remember the song that Sister Mary and I taught you — the one that goes like this . . .? (I made the organ sound like a calliope) *Um-pah-pah, um-pah-pah . . .*"

Without losing a beat, the dancers lined up in the sanctuary and started their disarming little ballet while the rest of us sang out the words:

Love makes the world go round,
Love makes the world go round.

Those simple lyrics, proclaimed and interpreted by our Life-I-Love-You children, provided us with an emotional bridge that allowed us to catch our breath and psychologically travel from the homilist's challenge to the celebrant's intonation of the solemn Eucharistic Prayer: "Lift up your hearts . . . Let us give thanks to the Lord our God." Once there, we gratefully celebrated the gift of Christ's Body and Blood — a Body sacrificed like that of the enemy soldier's but risen in ultimate victory, and Blood poured out for the remission of all the death-inflicting sins of the warring world.

Someone told me later that Father Avery Dulles, the famous Jesuit theologian and future cardinal (whose father was the former U.S. Secretary of State John Foster Dulles), had been sitting in the front pew throughout the entire series. When asked for an assessment of this final sermon, he is said to have replied, "If anyone had said that in words, I would have walked out of church!"

Two additional memories I cherish of that remarkable liturgy:

My little dog, Muffin, a Maltese terrier poodle, was selected to lead the motley procession of children, circus personnel and ministers into the church. She was wearing a ruffled clown's collar, and attached to her tail was a helium-filled balloon. Upon reaching the front of the altar, just as the final note of the gathering song had been sounded, as if on cue, she gave out this one fantastic, resounding yelp — as if intoning, "Let us pray!"

Lastly, at the Sign of Peace, as everyone went around greeting and hugging each other, I distinctly remember Father Nick Weber leaning over to one of his associates and whispering, "Can you feel the circus?" [By that he meant the Spirit.] I never forgot that remark because when Nick was a seminarian in Berkeley, he confided in me that liturgical rituals very often left him cold. Inexplicably, his spiritual nourishment came mostly from his circus ministry.

How stunning! I thought: *The new liturgical reforms can even convert a clown!*

On the following Monday, the bishop was informed that the principal celebrant at his cathedral had swallowed fire on his way out of church — with a live monkey on his back, that a clown had given the sermon, and that a dog had delivered the Call to Worship!

Furthermore, was he aware of the fact that the cathedral rector was in Seattle?

When the Reverend Monsignor returned from the Northwest, a letter was waiting on his desk. Among other prohibitions, it decreed that henceforth all animals were to be excluded from the Sacred Liturgy.

I couldn't believe it: my little Muffin, excommunicated!

Faces in the Revolution*: Delano farmworkers*

Faces*: concluding liturgy; photo of mime by John F. Lodato*

Chapter Five:

Ha-Ha-Hallelujah

In the winter of 1970, the parish was heartbroken. Father Jim Keeley, the "spark of St. Francis," had reluctantly agreed to become pastor of a parish in east Oakland. Several months later, Mike Lucid announced that he too would be departing; the Bishop had appointed him to head the department of Religious Education of the diocese.

These moves seemed to indicate that certain influential chancery officials were getting nervous about our experimental and admittedly creative interpretations of Vatican II reforms. Had we been stretching the rubrics or lack of them a bit too far?

Lucid was replaced as cathedral rector by the handsome and dashing Monsignor Joseph Skillin, thirty-six at the time, who was Bishop Begin's private secretary for the previous nine years. Had he been dispatched to his boss's mother church to keep experiments and innovations to a minimum?

The young prelate's personal inclinations, however, were altogether aligned with those of the "troublesome" staff. In fact, his charismatic personality and talented leadership would propel the parish into extending its innovative and creative energy to establish a parish council "with teeth." He also encouraged Holy Names Sister Maureen Delaney from the parish school to pursue special training as a community organizer and put her in charge of a neighborhood "community apostolate" which he declared would be our fourth priority.

It was Skillin's genius to provide a solid infrastructure for lay leadership to take root and thrive. A parish council was formed with seven "task forces" representing the parish's four priorities: worship, religious education, senior citizen ministry and community action (each with a hired staff person), and three additional concerns: finance, social events and youth activities. The chairpersons of these committees plus staff comprised an Executive Committee that set parish policy and made all decisions. The bylaws stipulated that the pastor was to have one vote and no veto power.

Skillin reasoned that as the council evolved into a competent and healthy agent of pastoral leadership, it would become an independent power base and effective counterbalance to clergy-dominated Chancery structures. In time he would be proven right.

But the talented monsignor was more than a corporate strategist. When informed of the theme for the forthcoming summer series, he chuckled with delight and insisted on joining the group of writers, liturgists and performers. It was a good thing he did, because the summer liturgies were about to get us into a lot of trouble!

Our objective for the 1971 July Summer Series was to reflect on and celebrate the spiritual, psychological and healing dimensions of "Humor," a characteristic that permeates the whole of human history, including that of the Roman Catholic Church.

The four-week series began with "A Serious Talk on Humor." Monsignor Maurovich returned to the pulpit, paired this time with a "live" panelist, Ray Orrock, a local columnist and humorist who provided the congregation with the following lyrics to be sung to the melody of the song "Supercalifragilisticexpialidocious," from the movie *Mary Poppins*. He called it "The Traditionalist's Lament":

Refrain: *Introibo, Tantum Ergo, Kyrie Eleison.*
Give me back my pamphlet rack and surplices with lace on.
If Catholic means rock-and-roll I'd rather be a Mason.
Introibo, Tantum Ergo, Kyrie Eleison.

I used to sing of Christ the King and goodly saints of yore;
But now some fool named Michael tries to row his boat ashore.
The Father, Son, and Holy Ghost have given way to trash;
The Trinity has been replaced by Crosby, Stills and Nash! (Refrain)

They say they dropped the Latin hymns 'cause they weren't understood;
And hymns that no one understands are neither wise nor good.
Well, I will stop my nagging and shut up my wagging jaw,
If someone will just tell me what is meant by *KUM-BY-AH*! (Refrain)

I fondly sigh that, when I die, no matter how I've sinned,
The choir will sing *Grant Him Rest* not *Blowin' in the Wind.*
And as I soar to heaven's door to rest among the stars,
Please bear me there with angel harps...not banjos and guitars!
(Refrain)

Ray Orrock's clever ditty clearly expressed the prevailing tensions within the Catholic populace. Pope John XXIII's *aggiornamento* (updating) had spawned changes, especially in the liturgy, that greatly unsettled many of the faithful, creating bitter divisions. It was precisely at times like this, Maurovich and Orrock declared, that the world gratefully welcomes the gift of humor. Without it one could hardly be saved. Human life and history are so tragic and absurd at times that only inspired satirists can make them bearable. These lighthearted seers provide the perspective and balance so necessary in maintaining one's mental equilibrium.

Imagine a world, they proposed, without the likes of Peter Sellers, Carol Burnett, Milton Berle, Alan King or Rowan and Martin! They are secular exorcists, they declared, exposing and dispelling the demons of disintegration and despair. How could one possibly understand politics, for example, or the scandals rocking the governments of the world, without these "jesters" who phrase things in the form of a joke because so much of what goes on *is* a joke? They place a mirror in front of our feeble and fumbling efforts to reveal the farce. They make us laugh at ourselves and in so doing restore the fun and the mystery to Life.

Our homilists concluded by suggesting that perhaps a good dose of humor would help in dealing with the current tension within the Church.

And so they announced that for the next three weeks the Cathedral staff would be combing the Scriptures for clues and guidance, and engaging a few Christian satirists, "exorcists" and "jesters" to provide some perspective and balance for the Catholic soul.

Thus the stage was set for the following Sunday's liturgy: a theological treatise on the virtue of hope, by the renowned theologian, Joseph Powers, S.J., who subtitled his presentation: "Life in the Pumpkin Patch: Looking for God with Linus."

Acknowledging the work of Charles Schultz in his *Gospel According to Peanuts,* and with the help of transparencies of Schultz's characters Linus, Charlie Brown, Lucy, Snoopy and the others, the eminent professor theologized on the necessity of patience and the salvific dimensions of friendship.

"What's the matter with us anyway? *[Cartoon: Linus in the pumpkin patch]* Are we spending too much time just thinking?

Are we looking at things from the wrong angle?

Are we missing something which is really very simple — but still very important? Are you really very close to us, just a little disguised?

[Snoopy in a magician's outfit]

But there is a way, Lord — a way which you have shown us.

There is a way to keep going — to keep us walking after you...

And that's the real miracle, the real revelation that makes all the puzzles in the world seem really simple.

You are the friend who makes doing things with our friends such a special thing...

[the cast of Peanuts characters on the ball field]

So give us more friends, Lord. Let us be friends together.

That's what we really are here for, isn't it?"

*****

At the conclusion of Fr. Powers' graphic reflection, a troop of actors from the San Francisco production of *You're a Good Man, Charlie Brown* scrambled onto the sanctuary and delivered a scene from the play, gingerly tossing around a softball as they exchanged definitions of the term "Happiness," breaking into the song of the same title.

"Happiness is morning and evening
Daytime and nighttime too;
For happiness is anyone and anything at all
That's loved by you."

*****

Not so the bishop!

No, sir! He was not happy that morning in the middle of July, when, unbeknownst to us, he slipped into the cathedral to show off his "masterpiece" to the dean of the Cleveland College of Arts. Upon opening the church door, he caught Steve Essig in the act of nailing to the walls of the curving redwood panel that spanned the entire length of the sanctuary a giant poster that spelled out in carnival colors the theme of our final Sunday's celebration:

"Ha-Ha-Hallelujah!"

It was Skillin who informed me that I had been summoned to the Bishop's Office. "Don," he said, "I lived with the man for nine years and have never seen him this angry! He's ordered me to take the banner down — right now."

"Don't do anything until I get back. I'm going to get him to let us finish the series."

"I'm afraid you won't be able to do that, but good luck, anyway."

Begin was sitting at his desk, looking down so that the fire in his eyes wouldn't consume the poor young liturgist in front of him.

"Just what do you think you are doing, Father Osuna?"

I did not let him finish another sentence. He'd asked a perfectly sane question and I was going to answer it truthfully: "Bishop," I began, "we are exploring the reality of humor as a God-given gift to help us cope with the tragedies and absurdities of life. We feel that the present turmoil in the world and in the Church . . ."

Begin exploded, pounding the desk with his fist, "Were they playing baseball in the sanctuary last week?"

"Why, yes, Bishop," I responded truthfully. "A talented group of actors were sharing some wonderful insights from a play by Charles Schultz, the creator of the Peanuts comic strip — you know, Charlie

Brown, Shroeder, Snoopy . . . The softball was just a prop . . . And before that, the people were shown Father Joseph Powers' profound commentary on the need to have patience and always stand by one's friends . . ." (I emphasized the last phrase: "stand by one's friends.")

I could see Begin's jaw unhinge in utter perplexity.

The fire, however, was still in the eye. "You will stop this nonsense right now," he demanded, looking me straight in the eye. "You will take down that banner and cease this nonsense!"

It was my turn to show some fire. Staring him straight in the eye, I shot back, "No, I am not going to stop the 'nonsense,' because to me and to the countless people who have spent weeks preparing these liturgies, it is not nonsense! It is a deeply religious and highly significant project — to which we have committed hours and hours of work. Nor will I be responsible for demoralizing the thousands of worshipers who have been flocking to your cathedral and who are enthusiastically awaiting the conclusion of this highly successful summer series. You will have to stop the 'nonsense' yourself by removing me from the cathedral staff!"

I detected a faint smile trying to emerge from his lips as he remarked, "Well, we'll get around to that in due time."

Then he sat back, breathed a sigh, thought for a few seconds in silence and said, "Very well, you can finish out the series, but I want some changes made in the future, is that understood?"

"Yes, Excellency. Thank you very much. You are going to make a lot of people very happy."

Driving home, I began to compose a few definitions of my own:

"Happiness is . . . winning a battle, if not the war!"

"Happiness is . . . narrowly escaping the same fate as your dog's!" (At least, I had not been excommunicated — not yet, anyway!)

On entering the rectory, I triumphantly informed Skillin of the bishop's decision. He responded, "I don't believe you!" Then he went upstairs and phoned the bishop, who confirmed the "green light." One could hear the roar clear across the street at the Greyhound Bus depot: "HA-HA-HALLELUJAH! . . . Back to work, Osuna!"

*1971 Summer Series on **Humor***

Staff entertaining at a parish vaudeville show

Chapter Six:

Vatican Two in Review

It's a good thing that Bishop Begin didn't ask what we had planned for the final liturgy — he would have closed us down on the spot! Months before, a team of writers and liturgists had been assembled and asked to analyze the current state of the changing Church. The group included clergymen, journalists and a couple of lawyers — all of whom were selected for their wit, comedic gifts and knowledge of Church issues. Their mission: Put your conclusions into the funniest available format.

One did not have to be a psychologist to recognize that the Catholic community at the time was suffering from a bad case of schizophrenia. Both the clergy and the laity were polarizing — and getting more aggressive as they drew apart. According to some cynical analysts, there were the "litniks" and the "throw-backs," the "high-churchers" and the "low-churchers," the "Traditionalists" and the "Vaticanist II-ists". Waves of priests and nuns, they contended, were petitioning for a dispensation from their vows or exchanging marriage vows with each other. The nuns who remained were exchanging habits for the latest fashions and *haute couture.*

Revisions of the Roman Ritual (official book of rubrics for all the rites) were coming so frequently that a rite for a baptism, funeral or marriage seemed to become extinct after its initial enactment. And within the Mass there were so many variations and options that one never knew whether the celebrant was following a new rubric or making one up.

Well, our talented team in downtown Oakland had a field day. They came up with a script to rival any by Rowan and Martin's *Laugh-In* troupe in "beautiful downtown Burbank."

It's just as well that copies of the completed script are nowhere to be found, and that the one single recording of the event has mysteriously disappeared. On paper, and even on tape, the event, while insightfully relevant, was nevertheless hilariously irreverent!

This is what I remember about the "creative celebration" of July 25, 1971: *A Catholic Laugh-In.*

My seventy-eight-year-old mother was sitting in the second pew. She would later tell a friend, "I'm so glad that Monsignor Skillin came out in the beginning and said what he said."

Dressed in full monsignorial magenta robes (those of a papal chamberlain), the gallant prelate sashays through the sanctuary like a model displaying the latest Christian Dior creation, twirling in the air one end of his tasseled purple sash. He approaches the microphone and greets the eleven hundred worshipers:

"In keeping with our theme, we are going to laugh at ourselves today and at the strange things that are going on these days in the Catholic Church. If anyone here does not have a sense of humor or believes that the 'sacred' cannot be approached with 'an unholy reverence,' then I invite you to leave now! You really don't belong here unless you can pray and smile at the same time." This in turn was the cue for the instrumental ensemble to intone the processional hymn and the cathedral choir to lead the people in song:

> When you're smiling, when you're smiling
> The whole world smiles with you.
> When you're laughing, the sun comes shining through.
> But when you're crying you bring on the rain,
> So stop your sighing, be happy again.
> Keep on smiling, 'cause when you're smiling,
> The whole world smiles with you.

The reading from Scripture echoed the opening anthem:

> Rejoice in the Lord always! I say it again. Rejoice! . . .
> The Lord himself is near. Dismiss all anxiety from your minds

Present your needs to God in every form of prayer
and in petitions full of gratitude. Then God's own peace . . .
will stand guard over your hearts and minds, in Christ Jesus.
(Philippians 4:4–7)

Ana Lee Daste, one of the choir's gifted altos, attired *à la* Lily
Tomlin, enters the sanctuary, seats herself at the telephone station, puts
on an operator's headset, inserts a cable and sings out:
"Good morning, Chancery Office . . . How may I direct your call?
You want to speak to one of our young priests?
I'm sorry, they are all on a leave of absence! . . . Hello? . . . Hello?
. . . *(ring, ring)*
Good morning, Chancery Office . . . You want to speak to Sister
Maureen? One moment, please, I will have to locate her for you . . .
please hold . . . *(inserts another patch)*
Hello, Saks Fifth Avenue? . . . Yes, I'm trying to locate Sister
Maureen. I believe she is in your beauty parlor having her hair dyed . . .
(Yes, ha-ha, from a Dominican to a Franciscan! . . .)
Oh, she's left . . . Oh, I see . . . she can be found where? . . . In the
bridal department! . . . Well!"
(And so on!)
"Have you heard that the Irish are finally implementing the liturgical
reforms? Yes, they are now saying the Rosary — facing the people!"
"Bishop Begin, call your office!"
(And so on!)
Out comes Skillin again, in his splendid raiment. He informs the
assembly that one of the most popular liturgical reforms of Vatican II
was the reinstatement of the Sign of Peace, a greeting rite just before
Communion, also called the "Kiss of Peace (*Pax*, in Latin)." However,
the ritual differed considerably in various countries of the world, as they
were about to witness.
The Cathedral Players (a group of amateur actors/parishioners
assembled and directed by head lector Jerry Johnson) proceed to
demonstrate:
First, the *British* Kiss of Peace, which consisted of a perfunctory
nod of the head and the extension of the index finger!

The *Italian* ritual was altogether the opposite: gesticulations of every sort until a buxom woman is heard to screech "*Bestia bruto!*" as she elbows the offending gentleman next to her.

For the *French* Kiss of Peace, a placard appears and is paraded about: "CENSORED!"

Finally, the *Irish* version:

Out comes this clerical "apparition" from out of the Tridentine past (John McDonnell), decked out in an ancient lace alb, moth-eaten "fiddle-back" vestments, and a three-cornered pompomed biretta (hat) that struggles to keep an unruly wig in place. Sacramentary (the "latest" book of rituals) in hand, he ambles over to the pulpit, leans over to the congregation and, in the thickest of Irish brogues, solemnly proclaims:

"As you know, dearly beloved brethren, our Holy Mother Church, in her infallible wisdom, has recently ordained, that, at this particular juncture in the Sacred Liturgy, all the faithful who assist at Holy Mass shall be invited to turn to one another, and offer the neighbor the time-honored gesture of love and affection among Christians called the *Pax* . . .

. . . And for your penance you shall say one Our Father and three Hail Mary's!"

"Bishop Begin, say your *Office!*"

William Shannon "Bill" Parrish, distinguished personal injury lawyer and later municipal court judge, came up with the brilliant suggestion of "planting" an indignant protester in the congregation who at the right moment would interrupt the proceedings and vociferously indicate that the limits of religious decency and propriety had been exceeded.

(Bill, by the way, was the one who had come up with the "Irish" punch lines!)

The team elected Bill to write the material and deliver it as well. He was perfect for the part — mature, silver-haired and respectable — and besides, he was a well-known member of the Oakland "Establishment."

So somewhere in the middle of a skit, probably the one on "Reloading the sacred Canons," a voice from the pews demands to be heard:

"Just one moment, my Very Reverend Monsignor . . . one blessed moment! This is going too far! Have you no respect? Where is your sense of propriety and decorum? Last year it was the circus and today betrayal, betrayal of all that is holy, genuine and sober! You make a mockery out of being a Catholic! Look at the lot of you! Ministers in makeup! This is not *my* religion, and I will not stay here any longer and watch you ridicule *my* Faith!"

With that, the indignant barrister steps into the aisle, reaches into his seat, and, with a matador's flourish, dons the flamboyant cape and feathered headdress of a Knight of Columbus. Producing the distinguishing sword of the Order, he unsheathes the weapon, brandishes it on high, and fervently parades down the aisle and out of sight!

"Bishop Begin, close your office!"

The End

Interestingly, the only response from the Bishop's Office was an interoffice memo from Julie Bandau, Bishop Begin's private secretary (and a Skillin supporter):

Bishop said to send you these letters.
Letters such as these make the M-I-L-E in "smile" stretch out of sight!
Remember . . . God Loves ya, and so do those who know ya.

Enclosed was a note to the bishop from a lady parishioner. It stated:

"One of the purposes of the Church as a community is to provide a mirror in which we can see our blind spots and our shortcomings. To this the staff of the Cathedral has addressed itself these past few weeks . . . I especially enjoyed last Sunday's "Laugh-In." It's good to see the church taking their faith more seriously than themselves . . ."

A lengthier enclosure bore the impressive letterhead: "Saint Mary's College of California *Office of the President.*" In it, the distinguished educator, Brother Mel Anderson, FSC, related that the countless priests, brothers and sisters from all over the nation who were attending the summer courses at the renowned Christian brothers' campus routinely made a pilgrimage to the Oakland Cathedral for Sunday worship, as he had been doing those past three weeks. "Some" he wrote, "will find aspects of the Cathedral [liturgies] enigmatic." But that would be because they were ignorant of the "stark realities facing us today." He concluded with the following observation:

It cannot be that people go to the Cathedral merely to be "entertained." Clearly it is not "entertainment" which draws multitudes, but the fellowship of Christians at worship together: praying, singing, smiling, and reflecting on the word of Christ expressing itself through realities men encounter in their daily lives . . . I am sure that the multitudes who appreciate what the Cathedral staff is doing will not only understand the meaning of Christianity more deeply, but will also find themselves working more effectively, with Christian insight, in the secular world.

Other written testimonials appeared that sought to underline the historical and spiritual significance of our liturgical efforts. The following excerpt is from *The History of St. Francis de Sales Parish, 1886–1986* written for the cathedral's centennial celebration by Jeff Lewis, former editor of *The Catholic Voice* (pp. 102–03):

Reflecting on St. Francis' "national and international attention," Frank Maurovich, managing editor of *Maryknoll Magazine,* emphasized that the Oakland Cathedral "was one of the first places in the world to successfully integrate the new liturgy of Vatican II."

"The Church has always maintained that the Mass was drama," he explained, "but few people realized how much drama was robbed from the Mass when the solemn and melodious sound of Latin was dropped and when the bells and bows and multiple genuflections were drastically lessened or eliminated. Turning the altar around and using the vernacular made it a whole new ball game, but most of us just moved from one to the other without any real preparation and were puzzled by the lack of response, by the flatness, and in some cases by hostility."

Praising St. Francis de Sales' creative and successful blending of word, music and sacrament, Frank credited the combination of liturgical talent and preparation. Recalling his own participation in a four-part summer series on "Faith and Humor," he commented, "I was asked to come to a meeting at the Cathedral at least two months prior to the series. Homilists, celebrants, and choir people were all represented and asked to give suggestions, while the general outline of the series was proposed." Noting that the   principal participants came together once again for more detailed preparation, Frank added, "the people involved were all talented and undoubtedly would have produced good liturgy without such extensive prior communication, but the actual result was not, in my opinion, good liturgy — it was superlative — because the existing talent was not only sparked and sharpened to excellence, but also blended in such a way that you could say 'the result was greater than the sum of its parts.'"

Montage of various "creative celebrations"

Montage of various "creative celebrations"

Chapter Seven:

Smooth Sailing . . . for a While!

Frank Maurovich was right about the amount of time we spent in preparing each liturgy. Whether it was planning an ordinary Sunday Mass, a special Advent, Holy Week, summer series or a special episcopal ceremony, we labored over every liturgical and artistic detail as required. The planning committee was called the Liturgy Task Force because it was entrusted with the "task" of formulating the nature and parameters of our worship services. Every liturgical ministry was represented: clergy, acolytes, sacristans, lectors, ministers of Communion, bread bakers, greeters, ushers, art and environment designers and musicians, plus a couple of at-large members.

First, the committee determined the theme of the service based on the nature of the occasion and the assigned scriptural readings. Next, the group agreed upon a homilist/preacher who could adequately develop the theme. Finally they discussed the possible use of "special effects" such as dramatic and visual enhancement. The task force's decisions were then entrusted to me as liturgist and artistic director to craft all the elements into an integrated celebration. As music director, I selected and arranged the music for the congregation and approved McDonnell's choices for choir and ensemble.

Some liturgies, of course, required more structuring and rehearsal time than others; but each service was expected to maintain the same standard of good worship and art. The important challenge for me was to make sure that every service expressed and inspired an experience of genuine prayer; that meant keeping the balance always in favor of prayer over artistic effect.

All the work and time the task force and liturgical ministries put into planning were evident in the positive and prayer-filled response of the worshiping community.

Any reservation Bishop Begin may have had regarding our liturgical efforts abruptly blossomed into full, unquestioned support as a result of an important liturgy that took place three and a half months after the *Catholic Laugh-In.*

The Federation of Diocesan Liturgical Commissions (FDLC) was to hold its national convention in San Francisco in October 1971. Priests, liturgists, scholars, chancery officials and bishops from throughout the country would be pouring into the City by the Bay with its recently constructed cathedral labeled the "Chartres of the West." It was a towering cruciform monument resembling a launching pad for a heavenly rocket booster. The soaring honeycombed interior revealed breathtaking vistas of one of the most beautiful cities in the world. Its modern cathedral is without a doubt an architectural wonder and a fitting temple to the God of the expanding universe.

To my unbounded amazement, I received a phone call from the convention planners asking to celebrate the convocation's principal liturgy at the cathedral in Oakland! "St. Francis de Sales — not at the Chartres of the West?" I asked in disbelief.

"That's right," I was told, "we want to worship with your people, in your space, which all of us agree is the most exciting in the country!"

Everyone, that is, but Monsignor Robert Hayburn, Ph.D. (Musicology), who was the music director of the Archdiocese of San Francisco, and also the designer of the recently installed gigantic Ruffati organ. "Oakland doesn't even have a pipe organ, for heaven's sake!" was his reaction when told of the "change of venue," adding sardonically, "Of course, one doesn't need a real organ to do Broadway musicals on Sunday mornings!"

To say that our San Francisco "hosts" were upset over the snub of their cathedral is an understatement. On the other hand (or should one say on the other side of the Bay), Bishop Begin could not have been more flattered. His remodeled "masterpiece" would be the focus of the nation's liturgical practitioners. His only reservation: "What kind of a liturgy was the cathedral staff preparing?" He winced when informed that he would not be able to preside from his "throne" because there would be a large movie screen in front of it!

The inspiration for the theme and images of the liturgy came to me as Joe Skillin and I were on a rubber raft in the Pacific Ocean off the Santa Cruz beach. We were enjoying a "staff holiday" in the California summer sun.

"Just when is this big convention Mass supposed to take place?" asked my shipmate.

"On Wednesday evening, October thirteen," I replied.

"Oh, that's right around Columbus Day, isn't it?" he remarked. (Columbus Day, October 12, is referred to by the Hispanic community as *Día de la Hispanidad,* a time to celebrate the Spanish heritage shared by peoples of the Americas.) That's when it hit me! Of course! Hispanic heritage! We will put together a creative celebration of the Faith first introduced to the "New World" by Columbus and his Spanish chaplains — a Faith that subsequently was adapted and reinterpreted by tribes from Canada to the northern tip of Chile. The result: a wealth of colorful traditions, devotions, images and religious trappings — a treasure trove of ethnic music and artworks to spare!

We reasoned that it would be good to remind the conventioneers, who were responsible for worship in the parishes of this country, that Catholicism in the U.S. is intimately related to Hispanic influences: not only because much of the land was once part of the Spanish colonies, but because so many immigrants from Mexico, Central and South America are members of our Sunday congregations. To appreciate the Hispanic religious culture of so many of our constituents could only enhance our efforts to tailor our liturgies to local realities.

Steve Essig, our "master visualist," came through with a series of richly detailed photo images depicting Latin Americans praying and worshiping in their native countries as well as here in the U.S.. The visuals served as an "overlay" or commentary upon phrases from the Old and New Testaments expressing God's formation of a "chosen people . . . a holy nation set apart."

Underneath the verbal script, the cathedral musicians performed a musical score that combined the rhythms and melodies of the American continents so powerfully that one could feel the blood rushing through the images on the screen. Two flutes intoned the first bars of the familiar folk tune "Un Canadian Errant," and from there the music traveled South through the mariachi hymns of the Misa Panamericana to the liberating sambas of Brazil.

One could only marvel at the exuberance of the Catholic religion as it donned the colors and costumes of each nation it evangelized, and absorbed the multicultural contributions of its native neophytes: Mexico, Cuba, Santo Domingo, Guatemala, El Salvador, Peru, Ecuador, Paraguay, Argentina, Bolivia, Arizona, Texas, California. As the Psalmist says: *Non fecit taliter omni nationi,* 'He has not dealt thus with any other nation' (Psalm 147:20).

In his homily, Father James D. Shaughnessy, director of the Murphy Center for Liturgical Research at Notre Dame University, complimented Bishop Begin for his hospitality and loyalty to the spirit of the Second Vatican Council. He remarked that, were it not for the liturgical reforms of Vatican II, so graphic and soul-stirring a proclamation of the Gospel as the one "that we just witnessed" would never have been possible. He went on to suggest that the Church of our day was being challenged, as Christopher Columbus had been, to sail forth into uncertain waters. Like that intrepid captain and his crew, the People of God must discover and explore a new world of ministry. He bade bishops and liturgists alike to be courageous navigators, keeping their destination in sight and sailing forward in gathering storms and following seas!

There were a few other highlights that made the liturgy memorable — all but one was carefully planned. The vestments for the presiding prelate and the stoles for the twenty-four concelebrants had been fashioned from "serape" fabric and brilliantly colored muslin by our dear "Tia Isaura," a local parishioner and seamstress. The litany of petitions called the "Prayers of the Faithful" was delivered in the different languages spoken throughout the two American continents. (To my knowledge this is the first time this had ever been tried.) The Offertory procession featured representatives from several nations, dressed in their native garb and bearing gifts unique to their region.

It was during this procession that the unforeseen event took place. Rosa Parra, our representative from Mexico, came up with an ingenious offering. Colorfully attired in the sequined skirt and blouse of a *China*

Poblana, she proudly carried in her arms an enormous clay *holla* (bowl) filled with enchiladas. But what was so unexpected was the unique, unmistakable, mouth-watering aroma that issued from the dish! Like incense, the scent of a Mexican kitchen wafted through the nave of the cathedral, penetrating olfactory nerves, reaching down into the pit of the stomach and unleashing the juices that stimulate unwanted pangs of hunger! Not an inappropriate reaction at the Lord's Supper!

The concluding song expressed the grateful reaction of the entire worshiping assembly. It was a rousing rendition of the theme song of the worldwide movement that originated in Spain called *Cursillos de Cristiandad.* The lyrics joyfully commemorate the glories of God's expansive multicolored creation. Here is an English translation:

De colores, bright with colors the rainbow is splendid with light and with promise.
De colores, bright with colors the birds of the air build their nests in the branches.
De colores, bright with colors the fields are arrayed with the glory of Spring
And a love bright with colors has found me with others around me that makes my heart sing!
And a love bright with colors has found me with others around me that makes my heart free!

After the Mass there was a lavish reception for our guests in the church hall. Thank God, the parishioners had brought lots of ethnic foods to satisfy the as yet unrequited hunger pangs induced by the fragrance of the bowl of enchiladas!

A private reception in the rectory was held for the dozen bishops in attendance, including the outgoing president of the National Conference of Bishops, James Malone of Youngstown. He had been extremely impressed by the experience, I was told, and spent the whole evening toasting his fellow Ohioan: "To Floyd and his magnificent fleet!"

All I remember is that by the time I arrived in the rectory all the bishops had left except Bishop Begin, who was cruising out the front door, two feet off the ground. His parting words to me as we "passed in the night" were these: "THIS IS HISTORIC!"

Hosting the FDLC at the Hispanic Heritage Liturgy, October 1971

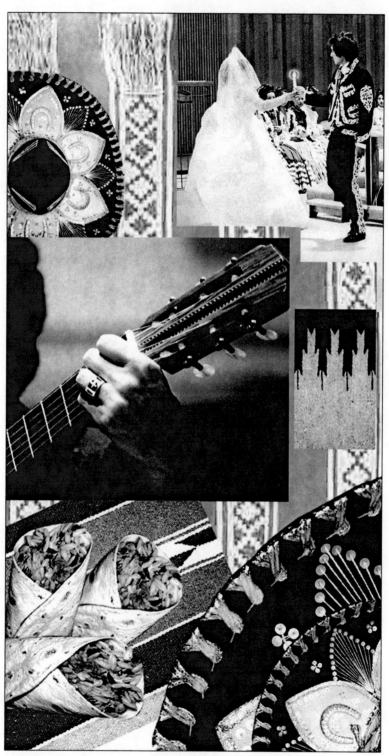

Celebrating Hispanic Heritage

Chapter Eight:

From Tenebrae to Transistors:
Electronic Music Comes to St. Francis

Mills College is a refreshing oasis in the middle of Oakland's eastern foothills. Originally a seminary for young girls, it had become a distinguished liberal arts college and had expanded to encompass a small male population in its exclusive graduate department. Its most famous alumnus is Dave Brubeck, the jazz pianist who was lured there by the prospect of studying under Darius Milhaud, the eminent French composer.

In the fall of 1971, I had been accepted into the new master's degree program in *Electronic Music and Recording Media* at the college's Center for Contemporary Music. Returning to academic life after ten years while still having to do duty in the "trenches" was an exciting prospect and a challenging opportunity. The idea of learning how to use Moog and Bugla synthesizers (recent inventions) and other mechanical devices along with film and television equipment was intriguing. Since liturgy is a synthesis of many arts, I reasoned, the new technologies for reproducing sounds and images might be useful in the service of worship. With some effort and a bit of creativity I might be able to introduce the new electronic arts into the liturgical arena.

I began to formulate my future master's thesis in terms of a liturgical celebration to serve as a performance vehicle. But, which one? It soon became clear that it had to be the Easter Vigil Service on Holy Saturday night — the most solemn ceremonial of the liturgical year.

This is what I wrote when I submitted the idea for a thesis project:

> Every worship service is a multimedia presentation of music, movement and visuals involving all the senses. Vestments, lighting, decor and ritual movement of ministers provide color and variety for the eye. The ear is constantly engaged in word, song or musical sound. The smell of flowers and incense filters the air, and the handshake of greeting makes one feel the touch of community. There is even consecrated food to refresh one's taste for the presence of God.
>
> Given such a rich medium, the artist can have a field day! But good liturgy — for all its artistic potential — is a heavy challenge, because worship is not essentially an artistic performance but an expressive affirmation of faith. Mystery is at the heart of it, and a response to mystery is its goal.
>
> But mystery, too, belongs to art, for art is the tangible, visual and/ or audial expression of an intangible and insensible reality. The goal of the liturgical artist is to shepherd all the arts into a spiritual and religious experience.
>
> Electronic music, with its unfamiliar sounds and inhuman qualities, carries a particularly strong ring of "mystery" for the average layman. As an art, therefore, it is tailor-made for religious services.
>
> In this thesis project, I will strive to effectively incorporate electronic music into the most solemn ritual of the Roman Catholic Church, the Easter Vigil Service, where the mysteries of Christ's death and rising from the grave are commemorated.

However, in order to produce and provide electronic music, one must have the appropriate equipment. So my thesis also included a proposal to "design, build and install a permanent quadraphonic sound system with a multipurpose control console for the Oakland Cathedral."

This was a formidable task and a challenging undertaking. Along with composing and creating the music itself, I would have to master the intricacies of electronics engineering in order to create a state-of-the-art audio system for the vast spaces of the Cathedral environment. Lastly, it would entail a significant financial investment.

"No problem," said Monsignor Joe Skillin, "let's go for it!"

Most people today take electronically produced music for granted. It is everywhere. Practically every movie and television score is currently produced by sophisticated synthesizers. Elaborate sound systems, installed in virtually every theater and performance hall, surround the audience with a battery of speakers that envelopes it in a sea of sound.

But in the early 1970s the electronics "industry" was just beginning to experiment with these innovations — as were we at the Center for Contemporary Music. However, as artists we were not interested in merely reproducing electronically the sounds of traditional instruments; electronic organs and preprogrammed synthesizers do that. Our focus was on exploring and unleashing the immense range of tonal possibilities that the physical phenomenon of an electric current is uniquely capable of producing. It was an entirely new musical system not based on the twelve tones of the West and far exceeding even the micro tones of Eastern modalities. Along with pioneers from throughout the world including Europe's *avant-garde,* we at Mills were exploring and giving shape to the music of the Age of Technology!

This was being accomplished for the most part by composing music on electronic devices, then transferring it onto magnetic tape, using the facilities of a recording studio and the advanced techniques of audio engineering and production. The tape became the "score" on which the music was inscribed and preserved for performance at a later date.

The piece that I composed in this way for my thesis was entitled "Christ's Descent into Hell," a subject that had captured my imagination since seminary days.

Of all the great solemnities of the liturgical year, Holy Saturday had always held a singular fascination for me. It is the only day on which no worship service is permitted (until the Vigil late in the evening). This is because Christ is in his tomb, dead, soon to be raised. And yet, Tradition has it that he was not inactive. According to Orthodox teachings, Jesus traveled to the underworld where all those who had been "justified" in ages past — Adam, Eve, Abraham, the patriarchs, the prophets, King David, all the saved souls of the Old Testament — were awaiting the appearance of the Savior. Wandering through the netherworld, the legend says, Christ called out their names, and led each one by the hand from the darkness of "hell" into the promised land of paradise.

This journey of Christ was the inspiration for my twenty-two-minute "tone poem" created on electronic machines, preserved on tape, and performed on the quadraphonic sound system custom-made for the Oakland Cathedral.

Paul Hertelendy, music critic of the *Oakland Tribune,* reviewed the event, April 23, 1973:

> The sounds of Easter are changing, even in churches where time-worn liturgy has been sacrosanct over centuries. One Easter vigil service in Oakland opened with the church cast into darkness. Slowly, out of the distance came faint sounds representing Christ's descent into hell. A muffled hum conveyed a sense of motion through nebulous ether. Occasionally a sound of what might have been distant voices in harmony and disharmony intruded, from ahead, from behind. And once or twice a faint glimmer of refracted lights flashed before us, as if to erode one's sense of time and reality.

> The listeners drifted through the gently mysterious sound environment during some 20 minutes of meditation and concentration, swept along gracefully in a medium few had ever encountered before. The music was literally inhuman, made not by instruments but transistors . . .

> The selection of electronic music for the Easter vigil Saturday night was ingenious. To depict scenes beyond our four-dimensional time-space continuum, the unfamiliar synthesized sounds invited one's suspension of reality . . .

> After the electronic meditation, conventional instruments and voices prevailed, but here too the sounds were a far cry from the plain chant and hymnody of yore...At the point of the service where the members

of the congregation greet each other, the music leapt over to the rhythmic, popular idiom and immediately a fairly formal group of worshipers transformed into a highly spirited communal body — a fascinating experiment in group dynamics, to say the least!

By the end, total strangers were smiling to one another, the joy of Easter reigned abundantly and no one (that I could discern) had left in protest . . .

Conveying the sensation of wandering about in the netherworld did not pose as great a challenge artistically as portraying Christ's coming from the dead back to life. That crucial juncture had me groping for an effective transition. Happily, I found a simple, "startling" solution.

Monsignor Skillin was to be the principal celebrant at the Vigil Service which followed on the heels of the meditation. So what I did was to splice onto the end of the tape Skillin's voice intoning the brief Call to Worship. It was recorded at very close range and broadcast over all four speakers at full volume. The shock was electric! After being "spaced out" for 22 minutes in a "mysterious sound environment," the audience's ears were suddenly assaulted by the familiar sound of a human being filling his lungs with air, and then in a loud, profound quadraphonic stage whisper, exhale a breath that formed the syllables "Let us pray!"

Everyone literally jumped out of their seats, stood erect, planting two feet firmly on Planet Earth! An experience of resurrection indeed!

Thereupon the main doors of the Cathedral swung open. In came the ministers and processional entourage carrying aloft the Paschal Candle. "Christ, our Light!" intoned the "live" voice of Monsignor Joseph Skillin. The assembly gratefully responded with the traditional "Thanks be to God!"

I, too, joined the thousand-member congregation, including the entire faculties of the Music Department at Mills College and the Center for Contemporary Music, in giving thanks to God for getting me through the "hell" of two years of graduate school!

What impressed so many of my colleagues from Mills was that I enjoyed the support of an institution that provided all the resources that an artist needs for experimental and creative work: musical elements such as a choir and instrumental ensemble, an eager and receptive audience, and the encouragement of a willing patron. It was also clear to them that as an employee of this faith community, I was expected to enrich its spiritual life by fostering and enhancing its worship. That was the key to the productive relationship.

After my graduation, the Cathedral continued its collaboration with the Mills faculty by commissioning several artists, local and European, to compose experimental works for its music ministry, and to explore the potential of the console I had designed for the performance of electronic music. In 1975 the Cathedral choristers and musicians produced their first album at the studios of the Center for Contemporary Music. It was called "Those Who See Light" after the popular hymn whose lyrics so aptly convey the Cathedral community's spirituality:

> Those who see light can walk in the dark;
> Open your eyes and see God.
> Those who look up will discover His face,
> Those who look down will uncover His path,
> Those who perceive God is here with us now
> Will see His return.
>
> Those who see light can walk in the dark;
> Open your eyes and see God.
> Those who have witnessed the sun rise and set,
> Those who have studied a flower unfold,
> Those who have focused on land, sea and sky
> Have seen Jesus Christ.
>
> Those who see light can walk in the dark;
> Open your eyes and see God.
> Those who see good in each person they meet,
> Those who look after their neighbor in need,
> Those who believe God is living in them
> Will see His return.

Text: E. Donald Osuna. Text and music © 1972, 1978, F.E.L. Publications, Ltd., Assigned 1991 to the Lorenz Corporation. All rights reserved.

Creating the "electronic tone poem" **Christ's Descent Into Hell**

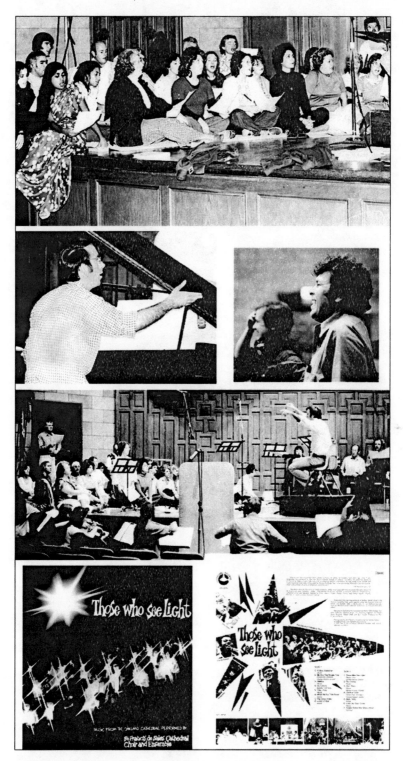

Recording session at Mills College, Cathedral Choir and Ensemble

Chapter Nine:

Zoos, Cages and Liberation

To celebrate my elevation to the rank of Master of Fine Arts, I and my classmate Tony Valdivia who had recently been invested as a Master of Science, exchanged academic robes for a pair of swimming trunks. Under a tropical Hawaiian sun and delicious trade winds, we savored our charmed careers and the national notoriety our diocese had attained over the past five years. Here we were, two sons of Mexican immigrants, ordained in the inaugural years of the Second Vatican Council, and fortunate enough to have successfully tailored its reforms to the church in the U.S. Valdivia recalled how at national conventions his hometown diocese was hailed as the "model of liturgical excellence." I, of course, was thankful that my ministry and talents had found an outlet and an acceptance far beyond my wildest dreams. Neither of us, however, ever suspected that within four months our moment in the sun would fade, and our beloved diocese would be shaken to the core by an internal scandal equivalent to a 7.5 tremor on the Richter scale.

*****

What happened was that the cathedral rector had fallen in love. Monsignor Joseph Skillin was in the grip of a monumental wrestling match with his conscience. It was the old celibacy issue which had been the bane of the Roman Church for centuries and had recently reared its ugly head. Following Vatican II, sexually repressed clerics, expecting imminent radical reforms regarding the prohibition to marry, awaited with bated breath a change in the Church's discipline. I knew of so many fellow priests who, like the cathedral rector, were hopelessly entangled in the maze of an intimate relationship and emotionally stymied at the prospect of having to choose between ministry and marriage.

Many left the priesthood silently and unnoticed. But, not Skillin: As rector of one of the most notorious churches in the country, the announcement of his civil marriage to a divorcee with three children became fodder for the tabloids.

It is uncanny how current concerns always found their way into our liturgies, and how hard-core issues were invariably reflected in our four-week seasonal celebrations. The 1973 summer series was no different. Originally it was to be called "Everything's Happenin' at the Zoo, I Do Believe!" after a Simon and Garfunkel hit song that in the opinion of our planning committee accurately described the state of the U.S. and of the Church. On national TV the Watergate hearings in Washington, D.C. were broadcasting the contortions of government officials, including President Richard Nixon, as they backed themselves into incriminating corners, unable to extradite themselves from past illegal activities. In Rome, Pope Paul VI was also finding himself maneuvered into untenable postures by adopting contradictory policies in order to placate the ever polarizing factions within the Church. As a result, bishops, theologians and the faithful alike were scrambling for protective shelter so as to salvage some semblance of spiritual sanity.

A zoo indeed! But in the end our liturgy committee renamed the series "Cages." The simple title suggested that everyone at one time or another works their way into a pickle, a jam or a hole — usually of one's own making. The good news, though, and the Gospel message we wanted to proclaim, was that Jesus had come precisely to free from bondage all those who were in the clutches of sin, sickness and death. The focus, then, of the four Sundays would be the person of Christ *the Liberator.*

We looked forward to hosting the usual summer crowds, including students and pilgrims from around the world, and celebrating with them the healing power of the Lord of the Sabbath! We were also delighted that Nick Weber, the Jesuit turned professional clown, would be returning to coordinate the final Carnival Sunday liturgy.

As usual, Fr. Weber's homily was memorable. It consisted of a telephone conversation between himself and "Helen the Hippo" who had just gone through a every exciting change in life style. "Just last week," Father Weber explained as he picked up the receiver to dial the liberated mammal, "she was moved from the San Diego Zoo to a new animal park near Thousand Oaks. The zoo she originally lived in was behind a moat in a very restricted area. At the new park life was very different."

Helen (depicted by a giant cardboard cartoon in the sanctuary) went on to trumpet the benefits of being freed from a caged experience to one where she was able to meet new friends and take on new challenges. Her parting words were:"I'm not used to having to think all the time, you know. Here there is always some decision to be made. We're always learning. But it's better this way. There's more work, more responsibility, and we're the better for it — praise God, my friend."

As an introduction to the Sign of Peace, the ritual greeting before the Communion Rite, Father Weber had two mimes come forward and perform a brief skit. The actors were obviously in adjacent enclosures, unable to touch each other. They frantically grope the imaginary walls looking for an opening. Miraculously one discovers a tiny hole and shows his neighbor how to find a corresponding one. Slowly, carefully, lovingly even, they simultaneously insert one finger into the aperture. The two digits touch. With that, barriers disintegrate, the two clowns embrace and scurry into the congregation to spread the "Kiss of Peace" — and freedom!

Shortly after that memorable celebration, we received an astonishing letter that corroborated my suspicion that these summer liturgies were powerful vehicles of God's transforming grace.

To the priests of St. Francis de Sales Cathedral,

Last April in Los Angeles my sister, who is, like myself, a convert to Catholicism, invited me to attend Good Friday services with her. I declined, saying something to the effect that it had been so long since I'd been in church, I preferred going to the Easter Sunday mass — for the living. She remarked that she understood how I felt. She said that in her mind one of the big differences between the Protestant Church we had both been raised in and the Catholic Church was that the Catholics had never been able to get Christ down off the cross. I am writing now to tell you that for the past three Sundays I feel that I have been privileged to participate in a celebration where Christ is not only off the cross, but down on earth — alive! I have also begun, for the first time in years too sad and lonely to remember, feeling Christ again — alive inside of me.

Because of certain circumstances in my life, I have been living in a "zoo." For the past three and a half years I have "caged" myself from other people, too frightened to even shake hands and speak to those around me in your church.

But this morning as those two young men so vividly portrayed my own apprehensions, I felt the iron bars of my own particular zoo start to crumble. I actually turned around and greeted other people with the hope that you have made me feel.

May I thank you now for healing my faith, restoring my hope, and making it possible for me to at least consider the receiving and offering of love.

S.D.W.

A week later, Joe Skillin bounded into my suite like a jubilant Romeo who had finally discovered the solution to a worrisome dilemma. "I'm going to do it!" he joyfully announced, "I'm going to get married." He would have preferred to continue wearing the Roman collar, he explained, but he now realized it was really a shackle around his neck.

Then he asked me if I would perform the ceremony. Startled, I asked him about his brother, a priest in a neighboring diocese: Wouldn't it be more appropriate for him to preside at the wedding? Skillin simply replied that his brother would not be available. The real reason of course was that his brother, a canon lawyer, well knew that any cleric officiating the marriage of a priest without a dispensation from Rome would be subject to suspension.

I then inquired where he planned to hold the ceremony. "In the cathedral" was the answer. I flinched. "Is that a problem?" he asked.

"Well, I certainly would feel more comfortable if it were held in a less conspicuous place," I replied.

"Then we'll do it at her parents' home," he conceded.

On Friday evening, September 14, 1973, I had joined my family for my eldest sister's birthday at the Sea Wolf Restaurant in Jack London Square. Just before dessert, I excused myself: "Sorry to leave so soon," I apologized, "but I have to perform a wedding." Fortunately no one asked any questions!

That was not the case, however, that weekend at the Cathedral when I announced that the pastor who had led us so ably for the past two years had gotten married! Nevertheless, the stunned and disbelieving congregation did take some consolation from my impromptu "toast" to the departed groom: "Monsignor Skillin's absence will only be a physical one" I assured the pained worshipers. "His spirit, vision and legacy will for all times remain embedded in these hallowed walls and in our grateful hearts."

As I finished the brief eulogy, I wondered if someone would be delivering one for me next week! If so, what would happen to this "awesome place?" What an irony, I thought: Skillin bursts out of his cage only to provide one for Osuna! Shall I willingly crawl into it? The consequences will be severe if they decide to slam the doors behind me. What to do?

We'll let the zookeepers decide!

1973 Summer series Cages

Exchange of the Sign of Peace

Chapter Ten:

The Prodigal: Not a Parable

The inevitable summons came a week later. Someone on the bishop's staff verified that I had been the officiating minister at the marriage ceremony and informed Bishop Begin. Shocked and disbelieving, he ordered me to his office.

"Where were you last Friday evening, Father Osuna?" he asked softly.

"Performing a marriage ceremony," I replied.

"Whose marriage ceremony?"

"Joe Skillin's."

Rising from his chair, he roared, "On whose authority!?"

"On the authority of the State of California," I responded boldly.

Stunned and caught off guard by the unexpected answer, the bishop recoiled. The intensity of his emotions, however, quickly rekindled his displeasure. "You have committed a grave sin! Canon Law requires that you go to Confession, make a public recantation, submit to—"

"I would never have consented to marry Joe if I thought it was morally wrong!" I interjected. "Frankly, I felt he had made a reasonable choice. I stood by him out of friendship —something my family taught me to honor above all things — we call it *amistad*."

(I chose not to say this to the good bishop at the time, but my action was based on the fact that Joe had decided to marry, as had so many other colleagues, in order to fulfill a basic human need and exercise a universal human right. Now that he had made his choice, I was not about to end a friendship over an issue one could consider legitimate, even though controversial.)

The disheartened bishop sank into his chair like a parent betrayed by a delinquent son. He stared at the intercom on his desk. After a few seconds he picked up the receiver and dialed the number of the adjoining office — that of his deputy and closest friend, Monsignor John P. Connolly, Doctor of Canon Law, Vicar General, Protonotary Apostolic, Financial Secretary and no fan of Don Osuna.

My career was over the minute Connolly entered the room and began his interrogation. Like a seasoned inquisitor, he knew exactly what to ask in order to secure my self-indictment and consequent termination as a priest of the Diocese of Oakland.

"Given the same circumstances," was the clincher in the carefully prepared litany of incriminating questions, "would you do the same thing over again?"

"Of course, I would," I answered truthfully.

At that point, Bishop Begin leaned forward and pronounced the inevitable sentence:

"Father Osuna, I have no alternative but to suspend you from the priesthood!"

Then he said something that surprised me because I had not informed him of any details about the wedding: "I understand that you persuaded Joe not to have the ceremony in the cathedral."

"That's right," I replied. "It took place at the bride's home."

To my greater surprise, he came around the desk, stretched out his hand, shook mine and declared, "I never like to leave without parting as friends."

The man had just ended my professional life and labeled me a canonical criminal without rights, faculties and paycheck! And he is my friend? It would take me three months to realize what a gift that handshake represented. It was something that only a wise and loving father could bring himself to bestow upon his prodigal son. What stayed with me during my exile were not the sanctions which the bishop had justly imposed, but the feel of his hand in mine as we parted. It was the same gesture we shared so many times at cathedral liturgies: "Peace be with you!" To offer me Christ's Shalom at this moment of banishment came to symbolize the handing over of the "portion of my inheritance" which I was unwittingly demanding and which by this gesture he was generously allowing me to squander.

I drove home in a daze and phoned my friend Tony to come and pick me up. "They've told me to leave the premises! I need a place to stay! They're sending someone to take my place! Come and get me! Hurry!"

An hour went by and no Tony! I looked out the window and saw a chancery official getting out of his car with a suitcase. *Oh, no! My replacement is here! Now what?*

I hurriedly grabbed some clothes and my little dog, Muffin, and fled by the back door. "We'll go to Ilda and Ed's (my sister and brother-in-law)," I informed my excommunicated companion. "They're out of town but I've got a key to the house." She just looked at me, sensing that something was very wrong. When we arrived at the house in Pleasant Hill, I collapsed on top of a bed. Muffin crawled under it. We slept for two days!

I awoke feeling like a mindless husband who had just been handed divorce papers and a restraining order; or, more accurately, like an adolescent who had finally achieved the independence he so longed for and now had no clue as to what to do with it!

Inspired no doubt by my guardian angel, I made another call. It was to a very special couple who I knew were always ready to take in strays from every walk of life — especially nuns and priests "in transition" and dogs of any denomination. With open arms, Bill and Colleen Parrish graciously offered us the "back house" on their rustic property in the Oakland hills.

Colleen Kelly was as bubbly as champagne and as heart-warming. Her Irish curiosity, humor and upbeat disposition enlivened and refreshed every relationship. Always ready to oblige, she was a perfect complement to her equally Irish husband. Bill Parrish was a brilliant Stanford-trained lawyer and a true son of St. Patrick when it came to conversation and conviviality. He became my mentor and subsequent "devil's advocate" during long talks after a day at work. One day, he decided I should be doing something useful with my life and time. So he got me a job as chauffeur and bailiff to his good friend, Lloyd Hudson Burke, Federal Judge, U.S. District Court, Northern District of California.

In the car and at home "over the bar," these two legal eminences conspired to persuade me to reconsider my "idealistic" [by that they meant immature] views of ecclesiastical issues including Canon Law. They suggested that I take a second look at my original profession.

I spent a couple of months listening to their arguments, which came down to one: All institutions are essentially flawed, including legal and religious ones. "To think otherwise is foolish in the extreme." Then, one day, I had one of those intuitive insights, an existential realization: The Church as we know it is not "without spot or wrinkle or stain of any sort" as had been proclaimed to me since childhood by parish priests and seminary professors. That, I would learn, is a biblical description of the Bride of Christ in her future final transformation through grace. The historical reality is that Mother Church is as much a product of human design as a creation of God. She develops in human history and is made up of human beings who by nature strive to create the kind of enterprises they want and need. Lonely Catholics organize bingo games because they want to socialize and play in a "safe" place; altar sodalities, Holy Names and St. Vincent de Paul societies, Serra Clubs, Legions of Mary, Knights of Columbus and countless other bands of believers recruit and marshal adherents in order to perpetuate a suitable brand of spirituality and foster appropriate works of charity. And the Catholic faithful everywhere subsidize the multi-billion-dollar empire of dioceses, parishes and religious congregations in order to secure for themselves centers of worship, learning, spiritual growth and social commerce that they hope will redeem their sinful souls. In the end, all these entities are subject to the rules of human psychology and politics because, for earthly creatures, there is no other way of behaving.

I remembered reading an article by Hugo Rahner (the brother of the renowned theologian Karl Rahner), in which he proposed that the truest test of one's faith in God is faith in the Church. And one could not claim to believe in the Church until one could envision, accept and cherish it as the "three-ring circus" that it is! The image is *Felliniesque* perhaps, but now I was beginning to see some validity to the thesis. Maybe I was having a crisis of faith!

I realized that for all of my life I had been idealizing the Church like a child his parent or a newlywed his bride. I had entered the seminary after sixth grade at the age of thirteen; it was still with a child's myopic vision and naive heart that at the age of twenty-six I promised to dedicate my life to religion. But it was to a "dream" that I had been wedded; the reality was an altogether sobering shock.

I knew that I could still reclaim my priesthood; all I had to do was comply with the six canonical conditions that the bishop had imposed (confession, public recantation . . . etc.). But did I really want to officially represent a "circus"? My mentors Parrish and Burke would answer: "Work for an imperfect church, or settle for a far more defective institution."

True enough. But what about one's integrity? What was the most authentic thing to do — the most honest? If I were to resume my life as a Catholic priest, I would have to consciously, willingly and genuinely embrace the role — and the Church, flaws and all — with open eyes and mind and heart, "for better or for worse, for richer or poorer, in sickness and in health, until death." I would have to abide by the rules, like them or not, and stand by policies and procedures that may not represent my own convictions. I remained hesitant.

I *was* sure of one thing: If I did go back, it would have to be to my community of St. Francis de Sales Cathedral. Despite human drawbacks, life at the cathedral was the closest thing to spiritual satisfaction and a nurturing environment that I could ever hope for.

*****

But would there be a Cathedral to go back to?

Stunned and disheartened by the loss of its pastor and associate pastor, the community had to confront the crisis of its own survival. "One Sunday the crowds were overflowing, the next week the cathedral was two-thirds full!" observed John McDonnell, cathedral choir director, whose foresight and dedication helped shape the Cathedral's music ministry from the start. "Those who belonged to the 'personality cult' that had grown around Skilllin evaporated overnight," he explained, "but the 'faithful remnant' continued to gather each weekend." His overall recollection: "It was a purifying experience!"

John Hendricks, president of the parish council and the one who is credited with keeping the parish from falling apart, offered this assessment: "The community was in a state of profound shock and disappointment.

The momentary impetus was to panic at Osuna's suspension — and at the appointment of Father Robert Fontaine, a conservative who was obviously sent to stop the entire parish in its tracks. However, the parish council was not about to let that happen; it would have to rally in order to hold the line. The new administrator would have to learn to live with us, not the other way around! Urgent meetings were called in order to organize the 'resistance' and strategize. I was assigned the task of having a 'heart-to-heart' with Fontaine." Henricks went on: "After several encounters, I discovered that he was intimidated by all the horror stories he had heard about the place prior to going there. Always the gentleman, he gave the impression of being very uncomfortable with the assignment. I'm sure he would have preferred to be in Tahiti!"

John McDonnell recalled that, shortly after arriving, Father Fontaine preached a sermon in which he compared the Church to a "kingdom" with the Pope as monarch, the cardinals as princes, the bishops as dukes and earls — and everyone else as "subjects." The entire proposition was utterly unsettling "in the era of Vatican II." McDonnell knew that the people in the pews considered themselves a "family" modeled on the Council's description of Church as the "People of God." No "regal emissary," he concluded, was going to disband that family without a royal fight!

And a fight there was! The staff and lay leadership (so carefully selected and trained by Lucid and Skillin) stood its ground and insisted that the structure and authority of the parish council remain as originally established. Accordingly, the determined members of the Executive Committee continued to manage all parish business without granting the new administrator any additional privileges other than those accorded the pastor in the bylaws, namely, one vote, no veto power.

Nor was Father Fontaine allowed to modify the most important element of the community's life — the liturgy. It was the quality and unique character of its worship that had originally created the cathedral community and it was its communal celebrations that inspired the worshipers to branch out into other ministries. Father Keeley had been vindicated — the people had learned to pray! For them the liturgy had become what the Vatican Council said it should be: "the source and summit of Christian spirituality." If the parish was to survive, its "heart and soul" would have to be safeguarded.

John McDonnell took on the challenge, assigning homilists, selecting and preparing all the music, and in general stage-managing all liturgical celebrations. He was especially sensitive to the members of the large cathedral choir and ensemble who were the backbone and engine of liturgical performance and participation. As a group and as individual musicians, they enjoyed a special rapport with Skillin and Osuna, and were particularly upset over their departure. For their sake, as well as that of the demoralized congregation, McDonnell persistently lobbied the Chancery for the quick reinstatement of Osuna whom they still considered their associate pastor and music director. Thus, McDonnell and the parish council successfully guarded against an immediate "hostile takeover."

The new administrator proved incapable and unwilling to confront such highly committed individuals and so determined a group of parishioners! Moreover, there was the cathedral staff to contend with: the nuns that taught in the school, the sisters that oversaw the ministries and the priests who presided at the sacraments. In the face of such overwhelming opposition, the beleaguered administrator grew increasingly reclusive, taking refuge in the carpentry shop he had set up in the bowels of the cathedral basement.

It was reported that when Bishop Begin first approached Father Fontaine about going to the Cathedral, he assured him that the assignment would not last more than a year — "until a permanent replacement is found." However, the story goes, every prospective candidate refused to go to the Cathedral "unless Osuna were out of the picture completely."

As a result, a holding pattern developed. The parish council flexed its muscles and stood its ground with growing assurance and strength. The chancery authorities maneuvered for time to come up with a "compromise resolution" and avoid an unpopular showdown. The standoff lasted up to Christmas Eve, 1973.

Early on the morning of December 24, 1973, I received a phone call from Father Brian Joyce, diocesan chancellor and seminary classmate.

"Don, the Bishop has asked me to inform you," he said hesitantly, "that should you decide to return to the active ministry, you will not be reassigned to the Cathedral." In other words, along with the previous six conditions for reinstatement he has added a seventh!

"Well, you can tell the Bishop," I responded with a hint of panic, "that if I ever do decide to go back, it will have to be to the Cathedral, or I won't be going back at all!"

"Would you like to talk to him about this?" Brian asked expectantly.

"Yes," I asserted. "I would be willing to negotiate this 'seventh' condition."

"I'll call you right back."

Five minutes later, Brian reported that the bishop would see me that same morning at his residence at 11:00 a.m.

At the appointed hour, I rang the doorbell at the mansion on Seaview Avenue in Piedmont, an exclusive enclave in the hills above Oakland. Sister Lydia, one of the bishop's two housekeepers, let me in and said that the bishop was waiting for me upstairs in his private suite.

The relaxed prelate greeted me cordially and pointed to one of his easy chairs.

"I understand that you are willing to return to the Cathedral," he began. Without giving me time to respond to what I thought was a question, he continued, "Well, I have contacted the cathedral administrator and he has no objections to your returning as associate pastor."

He finished his statement and waited for my response. For a good minute or so, nothing would come out of my throat. Then I heard a strange voice eerily echoing around the room. It was mine, and I was saying, "Well, in that case, I'll go back."

Abruptly the bishop stood up, came over to where I was now standing and embraced me.

"What do you drink?" was his next question.

"Gi-gi-gin," stuttered the same strange voice.

He laughed and, with genuine amusement, asked, "When did you learn to drink that stuff?"

"Ever since you consigned me to the inner city," I replied, regaining my composure and my vocal cords.

"Call your mother," he ordered as he sauntered over to the wet bar.

By the time I had finished dialing my mother and had her on the line, the bishop was taking the receiver from my hand, replacing it with a tumbler of Tanqueray, and jubilantly caroling into the mouthpiece: "Mrs. Osuna, this is Bishop Begin. I want to let you know that your son will be concelebrating Christmas Midnight Mass with me tonight at St. Francis de Sales Cathedral!"

I couldn't believe what I was hearing! No mention of sanctions, no requirement to confess, no promise to do penance! Just an embrace, a ceremonial toast, an invitation to Eucharist! It was like walking into a surprise party. What was going on — the replaying of an ancient parable? Was such paternal prodigality possible?

Top: Wm. "Bill" Shannon Parrish, host to departing 'prodigal'

Christmas Midnight Mass, 1973: return of the 'prodigal'

Chapter Eleven:

Return and Restructuring

The story of my reinstatement unfolded like a page straight out of the Gospel.

Midnight Mass on Christmas Eve, 1973, had been a memorable celebration: The bishop and hundreds of jubilant parishioners and friends toasted the return of their prodigal priest. But the real evangelical feast — with "fatted calf," music and merrymaking — took place thirteen months later, when, to everyone's surprise and the chagrin of a few, Bishop Begin announced my nomination as cathedral rector!

One priest on the bishop's staff was so outraged by the appointment that he instigated a letter-writing campaign requesting the Apostolic Delegate (the pope's representative in the U.S.) to rescind the bishop's action. (It was the same chancery official who had uncovered my complicity in the "Skillin Affair," and had leaked the story to the press.) Then, in an ultimate display of indignation, the irate cleric threatened to resign his post. The fatherly bishop is said to have replied with the words in St. Luke's parable: "We must celebrate and rejoice, because your brother was dead and has come to life again; he was lost and has been found." (15:32)

With all the pageantry of the parable and the panoply of the season, my installation as rector of St. Francis de Sales Cathedral took place on

Easter Sunday, March 30, 1975, the twelfth anniversary of my ordination
to the priesthood, and one month short of my thirty-ninth birthday.

*****

The first thing I did after assuming the new position was to inform the
flock that from now on "*all* of us would all have to behave ourselves!"
I suggested that in gratitude for "recent unexpected developments,"
we might make some conciliatory gesture — like complying with
prevailing liturgical protocol and "refraining from taking Communion
in the hand" — an ancient practice that many parishioners had adopted
but which was not as yet sanctioned by Rome. (The very concept of
a lay person touching the sacred host was "disrespectful," according
to the anti-reformers.) The offending communicants gladly complied,
sensing correctly that the request was more of a temporary tactic than a
permanent rubric. The bishop was pleased by this "token" of submission
to authority and by our willingness to restrain what he called "a recurring
penchant for anticipating future reforms!"

My next task was to reorganize and supplement the pastoral staff.
Father Jerry Kennedy of the Bishop's Office, who had lived with us
through the years of "transcendence and turmoil," stayed on as priest in
residence. He urged me to contact a Father Tom Ryan, a Marist priest from
Philadelphia who had surfaced during my absence and had thoroughly
charmed the cathedral community with his bubbly personality and
provocative homilies. "Tom Ryan," Kennedy insightfully insisted, "will
provide a missing ingredient and restore a certain 'sizzle' to the team!" I
phoned Tom in Georgia, where he had been assigned after his sabbatical
year in Berkeley. I invited him to return to California as my associate
pastor. His response was immediate and enthusiastic: "I'm sure that I
can convince my superiors to send me back to the hottest sanctuary in
the county!"

As luck would have it, two other "wise men from the East" came
looking for room and board in exchange for weekend parish work. Both
were on sabbatical in Berkeley. Father Theodore "Ted" Crone was a
young Sulpician professor pursuing a doctorate in economics, the other
a learned cleric by the name of Father Jack Miffleton, of Richmond,

Virginia, a gifted composer and specialist in literature and children's liturgies. So, in the fall of 1975, this talented trio from the East laid their precious gifts at the doorsteps of the tired and tested team from the West. Their generosity would open up for the staff and for the cathedral community exciting and imaginative horizons.

At the same time, these students of Berkeley's Graduate Theological Union (GTU) reinforced the ties that the Cathedral had already established with the Jesuit and Franciscan Schools of Theology. (Over the past several years, they had provided us with a continual stream of memorable homilists and liturgical performers.) The rest of the staff, which consisted of the nuns who taught in the school and the sisters who ministered to the elderly, the neighborhood and the school of religion, were delighted to welcome such a handsome addition to the parish pool of workers.

Fittingly enough, the 1975 July series was entitled *Getting It All Together.* Our aim was to address and celebrate the dynamics of "Conflict and the Mystery of Christian Reconciliation." The country after Watergate and Richard Nixon's resignation was crying out for healing. So was the Catholic Church, which continued to be pulled apart by increasing factionalism in the waning years of Pope Paul VI. At the same time, the world at large was turning to the eastern religions for insight and inspiration. People everywhere were seeking out personal gurus to point them toward the path of spiritual integration and peace. Our liturgy committee felt that Jesus and His Gospel outlined a compelling perspective on the subject.

As worshipers filed into the cathedral that first Sunday of July 1975, they were greeted by one of our liturgical designer's more breathtaking fabric-creations. Patricia Walsh had draped the sanctuary with a voluminous white veil that was split in two and fanned outward from the bishop's throne over the main altar like two arms embracing everyone in the space. In his keynote homily, the popular Berkeley theologian Joseph Powers, S.J. explained:

> Scripture speaks often enough about the fear which the people of
> Israel had for their God. He dwelt behind the veil of the Ark and only
> the leaders of the people or their priests could go in before him. When

they settled in the land and became a kingdom, they built a temple for
the Lord, and in the temple they hung a veil over the Holy of Holies,
hiding the Glory of God's presence from everyone except the priest.

But one day there came along a man who went about the land speaking
of God in a different way . . .God began to take on a human face and
to show himself in a new way. One day that man hung on a cross
outside the gates of Jerusalem . . .And as the last drop of his life seeped
from his broken body, he let out a great shout — a shout like the cry of
the victorious armies of Israel — a cry which signaled the downfall of
everything hostile to this God of love.
.

And at that cry, God burst from behind that great temple veil. He tore
it in half, from the top to the bottom. He flew from the Temple, flew
with a Father's love into the arms and heart of his beloved Son and
raised him up to be Lord and Christ. And bound into the limitless love
of their one Spirit, they set up their abode of Glory in the strangest
of places — in the depths of your life and mine — to bring to us the
splendor and power of this mystery of love and reconciliation.

The combination of these vivid visual and verbal images was
a stunning reminder of how the arts of sight and sound reinforce
one another and imprint a lasting impression on one's memory. This
happy marriage of eye and ear, icon and Gospel, would continue to
be a highlight in our liturgical experimentation. And Patricia Walsh's
environmental artistry would continue to interpret, enliven and enhance
the spoken images of the Scriptures.

Four weeks later, the series concluded on "Carnival Sunday" with a
contemporary parable written and narrated by Father Mike Moynahan,
S.J. and performed by his youthful and exuberant troupe of novices
from the Jesuit Novitiate in Santa Barbara.

The staged homily was entitled *The Kingdom that Was One* and told
the tale of the gentle "Prince Shalom," who had taught his subjects to
trust one another, accept their differences and lovingly care for each
other. Most important, "Shalom had shown them how to look deeply
into the eyes of every creature in the kingdom and see themselves."

However, one day when the good Prince had left the kingdom, his wicked cousin, the "Evil Escargot, prince of darkness and magician of the blackest arts," snuck into town and began sowing the seed of discord, "determined to develop deadly divisions . . . catastrophic carelessness, and in general screw up and demolish the unity and happiness of the tiny kingdom!" Escargot's *coup de grace* was to pass out to each inhabitant a pair of sunglasses so that one could no longer clearly peer into another's eyes. And so it was that the Evil Escargot taught everyone how to hide behind a "veil of tinted glass!"

Of course, Prince Shalom returns and encourages his repentant subjects to remove the obstacles that his cousin had maliciously put in their way and teaches them how to "look long and deeply into each other's eyes until you see yourself again in every creature."

The message of the series as a whole was that the path to integration and the "perfection" called for by Jesus is a continuous process of renewal and "conversion" — much like John XXIII and Vatican II's agenda for the Church. It can never be a one-time achievement. A lesson I was about to learn.

No sooner had I thought that the parish was back on track when a major crisis occurred regarding the parish school. For a neophyte in the art of administration, it proved to be a baptism by fire!

As a member of a coalition of five inner-city parishes, we had agreed to commission, participate in and abide by the conclusions of a study regarding the "physical integrity and security" of our school facilities. To our shock and dismay, the results showed that the St. Francis de Sales school building was "totally unsafe in the event of a significant earthquake." When the news reached the parents of our students, they panicked and were threatening to keep their children from classes. Along with the faculty, they demanded that we demolish the old school and build a new one — NOW!

So off I went to report the situation to Bishop Begin. I knew he would not be pleased with the news, but I never expected him to react so vehemently.

"Who authorized this study?" he fumed, pounding his battered desk.

(I sidestepped the question because the person who authorized the study was none other than the bishop's own financial secretary,

Monsignor J. P. Connolly. He had also paid for it with a diocesan grant of $3,000!)

"Let me tell you something, Father Osuna," the bishop continued. "In matters of this nature, one has to have faith!" Then, to my astonishment, he went on to "confide a secret" that he had kept from all but a few of his closest confidants: "When we were about to remodel the cathedral," he revealed, "the engineers counseled me not to do so because, according to their studies, the building would never withstand a major earthquake. I told them that was nonsense! Nothing will happen to God's temple as long as one has *faith*! Now, you go back and tell your people," he sternly ordered, "that they don't need a new school. What they need is faith!"

It soon became apparent that "faith" was not an option; there was no other choice but to tear down the school because of the compelling nature of the seismic study and the determination of the parents not to allow their children to be housed in an unsafe building.

I went back to the bishop and formally requested that the diocese demolish the present building and put up another so that we could continue the important work of educating the disadvantaged children of the inner city.

"How many of those children are Catholic?" he inquired.

"About thirty percent," I replied.

"And how many of the seventy percent of non-Catholic children are converting over to the Catholic religion?"

"One or two a year," I surmised.

"With statistics like that, one cannot claim to be running a *Catholic* school! I do not see any value in subsidizing a private academy!" he declared adamantly. Then, surprisingly he added:

"What I *will* do, Father Osuna, is build you a new community center complex — and the diocese will pick up the entire tab."

"That's a generous offer," I replied, "but I will have to put the issue before the parish council and the school folks."

"Well, keep this in mind:" he warned. "If they insist on a new school, they will have to pay for it themselves. No assistance will be forthcoming from this office!"

I was not surprised that the parish council strongly reasserted its commitment to education — a priority that from the beginning had been second only to worship. Nor was I shocked that they soundly and forcefully rejected the bishop's offer of a community center. Instead, they resolved to put up a complex of mobile units as temporary classrooms. After calculating all available and "raisable" funds, they pledged to spend a total of $95,000 on the project. (I thought to myself, *Talk about having* faith!)

We all watched with unspeakable sadness as the wrecking ball leveled the old red brick schoolhouse whose halls had not only welcomed our children but had hosted all our parish socials.

A verbal agreement was made with a contractor who claimed he could install a cluster of portable classrooms for $98,000 — a sum that was admittedly extremely cheap. However, two days before the required signing of the final contract, the Chancery lawyers discovered that the gentleman in question was about to be indicted by the federal government for fraud and tax evasion!

Realizing that our unilateral decisions had left us in an embarrassing position *vis-à-vis* the bishop, I searched for some face-saving maneuver to salvage our dignity, which was about to enjoy the same fate as the school's. I decided to use an approach that had proven successful in another famous "tug of war." It had been reported that during the Cuban Missile Crisis, when things were at an impasse, Bobby Kennedy suggested that the President simply ignore Kruschchev's second letter (which contained unacceptable conditions) and deal with the despot as if the document had never been received. So, in a final interview with the bishop, I acted as if nothing of significance had transpired since our initial meeting three months before.

"Bishop," I said in my most diplomatic tone, "on behalf of the people of your cathedral parish, I want to thank the Diocese for its generous offer to build and pay for a new community center complex at the site of the former cathedral school. We gratefully accept."

The bishop smiled then broke into good-natured laughter. He summoned his financial secretary who confirmed that the Diocese could provide a new center for about $325,000!

We concluded with a handshake that this time cost the bishop more than it did me!

The community was devastated by the fact that there would no longer be a school, as were the Sisters of the Holy Names, who had staffed the institution for close to a hundred years. Fortunately, however, several of the nuns agreed to stay on through yet another transition. Two of them established a temporary school, which they called Early Childhood Learning Center, in a rented building not far from the cathedral site. Sister Rosemary Delaney, the seventh-grade teacher, chose to join her sister, Sister Maureen Delaney, who headed our ministry of outreach to the neighborhood. In turn, the "dynamic Delaneys" hooked up with Father John Bauman, S.J., who was spearheading a grassroots community organizing movement that promised to rally the dissatisfied citizens of Oakland and successfully changing the complexion and quality of life in the poorer sections of the city.

As a result of their efforts and superb leadership, our new Cathedral Center became exactly that — a center for the community. The team conducted strategy sessions, neighborhood meetings, and training programs for developing in residents the skills needed to articulate social issues and effectively pressure City Hall to improve the living conditions in depressed and neglected areas.

So successful were they in establishing good relations with the political elements in local government that, within a year, citizen groups organized by the nuns had persuaded the City to close off the street in front of the cathedral and construct an expansive park-promenade. I was assigned the task of talking the bishop into contributing $75,000 to the project. In return, the area would be named *Bishop Floyd L. Begin Plaza.* It would be a fitting memorial to the founding bishop of the Diocese of Oakland, who upon turning seventy-five would shortly have to submit his resignation to the Pope.

But, on April 26, 1977, a few days before his retirement and three months before the completion of the handsome square, Bishop Floyd Lawrence Begin died.

Shortly before the bishop's death, John McDonnell and I had invited him to preview the Cathedral choir's recently recorded album, *Those Who See Light.* We played it for him over the quadraphonic sound system in the cathedral that he had so bravely remodeled and which had successfully become the "model of liturgy" that he had hoped for. The cream-colored walls and vaulted ceiling came alive, echoing the songs and sounds that had inspired so many worshipers from around the world to sing of the Spirit who "renews the face of the earth." Begin strolled pensively up and down the aisles of the empty nave swaying to the rhythms of the familiar melodies. When the tape ended, he came over to us, obviously moved. In a particularly tender mood, he surprised us by telling us about the first time he had fallen in love as a youth with a young girl from Cleveland. She entered the convent and he the seminary. He never saw her again. The music had reminded him of her!

McDonnell and I both had the same thought: *What a beautiful thing for our music and these precincts to be a springboard into a person's heart where ancient loves still breathe and cherished memories survive.*

We concluded our visit by presenting the bishop with the original manuscript of the score* to the piece I had composed for the dedication of the remodeled cathedral. The lyrics were as follows:

> *Introit for the Dedication of a Church*
> *O how awesome is this place!*
> *This is none other than the house of God.*
> *This is the gate of heaven.*
> *And it shall be called the court of God* (Genesis 28:17)
>
> *How lovely is your dwelling place, O Lord of hosts.*
> *My soul yearns and pines for the courts of the Lord.*
> *My heart and my flesh cry out for the living God.*
>
> *Even the sparrow finds a home,*
> *And the swallow a nest*
> *In which she puts her young:*
> *Your altars, O Lord of hosts.* (Psalm 84:3,4)

---

* The composition is scored for mixed chorus and an instrumental ensemble of harp, flute, organ, strings, brass, electric guitar and bass, chimes and tympani.

Top: Bishop Floyd L. Begin installing Osuna as cathedral rector.
Center: Joseph Powers, S.J. Bottom: William Cieslak, OFM Cap

Jesuit Novices and **The Kingdom of At-Onement** *liturgy*

Chapter Twelve:

From Pyramid to Circle

In the name of the Begin family I'd like to thank all the wonderful people in Oakland who were so kind to the bishop and so kind to our family. Among those special people are Father Osuna, the choir, and the Cathedral instrumentalists who have truly helped us to pray better. What greater service can anyone give. Nowhere else in the world is there a liturgy like you have here! (Father Daniel Begin, at funeral services for his uncle, Bishop Floyd L. Begin)

Among the mourners at Bishop Begin's funeral was John S. Cummins, auxiliary bishop of Sacramento, a native of Oakland, and the rumored successor to his hometown see. As Begin's first chancellor, the fifty-one–year-old prelate was intimately acquainted with all that had transpired in the diocese since its inception in 1962, including the unfolding of the "cathedral phenomenon." He sympathized with our reformist philosophy and inclusive vision — attributes that resonated with his large and liberal intellect, his gregarious nature and his outgoing personality.

After the interment, I sidled over to the six-foot-four former seminary athlete and *summa cum laude* graduate. "John," I whispered, "if you are named our next bishop, I invite you to come and live at the cathedral rectory."

He brandished his "First Communion smile" and, with an Irish twinkle, replied, "We'll cross that bridge when we come to it."

A week later he phoned from the state capital, accepting the offer. "Time to make the crossing!" he trumpeted.

The new bishop's decision to sell the Piedmont mansion and move the episcopal residence to downtown Oakland was greeted with applause by the public at large. The staff and parishioners of St. Francis de Sales cathedral parish were ecstatic — and flattered. The gesture constituted an acknowledgment and recognition of our progressive efforts and an obvious endorsement of our vision of Church. For the people of the inner city, it represented the bishop's desire to establish a closer and more visible presence within the city.

To accommodate the bishop's personal and social agendas, I undertook the remodeling of the rectory with the help of interior designer Jane Woolsey, who supervised the extensive renovation. Although costly, it was a justified expense, I felt. After all, several hundred thousand dollars had accrued from the sale of the Piedmont mansion; besides, we would be saving the Diocese a lot of money in property taxes, personnel expenses (gardeners, housekeepers, and so forth), not to mention utilities and maintenance costs. As if by magic, the unassuming three-storied brick building on 21st Street became a tastefully appointed residence and a place of hospitality and entertainment for a constant stream of local guests and an array of visitors from around the world. It became a welcome home for what had become the heart of the Diocese.

As might be expected of the bishop's "landlord," my personal routine was rearranged as well. Along with my regular parish duties, I took on the task of episcopal host and maître d', stage-managing the convivial bishop's domestic social calendar and supervising his countless dinner parties. But the most challenging role I faced was that of roommate/confidant and in-house sounding board. Like that of everyone in high authority, the bishop's life was an odyssey of Homeric proportions, including administrative, diplomatic and political adventures that would have vanquished the physical and emotional stamina of a lesser man. But, not that of John Cummins. In fact, at the end of a typically busy day he would come to my suite, pour himself a glass of brandy and proceed to verbally relive the day's experiences: rumblings from Rome, current labyrinthine developments within the diocese, pending decisions, ecclesiastical gossip and not-for- publication rumors. Most of the time, I sat in fascinated silence. On occasion, however, I felt compelled to speak up. Instinctively, I would offer an observation or opinion that usually reflected the views of my confreres "in the trenches" or the people in the pews — parties often overlooked and ignored by professional ecclesiastics. My spontaneous interventions proved helpful to a skipper who depended mainly on a crew of institutional officers. A little feedback from the people in steerage, I reasoned, would help the captain plot a steadier course!

The staff and lay leadership also had to adjust to the new bishop's position within the parish family. For the most part, we melded painlessly — with the exception of one minor crisis. The incident, however, served to clarify my relationship with the bishop and my responsibility to the people of the parish.

One of our focal concerns and proudest achievements had been the integration of women into all of our established ministries, including the highly visible and officially exclusive male ministry of *acolyte,* the official designation of one who assists priests and deacons at liturgical services. For years, half of all our altar servers were female volunteers who, like their male counterparts, had been trained, commissioned and invested with the white alb of their ministerial office. Although the Vatican had allowed women to read the Scriptures and distribute Holy Communion at Mass, it had excluded them from ministering in the sanctuary as acolytes.

At one of our late-night conversations, I asked the bishop if there were any items that particularly concerned him about "the way we do things around here." To my dismay, he replied that there was only one: He would feel more comfortable when presiding at liturgy if there were no women assisting at the altar. Personally he approved of their inclusion in ministry, he explained, but in view of prevailing church legislation he felt compromised and uneasy. "There are more substantive issues over which to go to bat," he declared, "should Rome decide to play hardball!" I informed him that the matter would have to go before the liturgy committee and the parish council. "As you well know," I reminded him, "*they* make all decisions around here — I have only one vote!... Furthermore," I was forced to acknowledge, "if the consensus goes against your request, I will have no choice but to side with the parish leadership. I hope you understand my position." He blinked, smiled and poured himself another brandy.

Neither the liturgy committee nor the parish council, of course, would hear of excluding women or "any other human being" from any parish ministry! So, at every liturgical function there continued to appear white-robed women proudly processing throughout the nave.

The only time I overrode the council's decision in this matter was when Pope Paul VI died in August of 1978. A major television network requested permission to film the memorial Mass for the deceased pontiff at which the bishop was to preside. The Oakland Cathedral service was to be part of a nationally televised broadcast. *How charming!* I thought, *Our liturgy is about to be exposed to the manipulation of TV directors and their zooming lenses!* That's when I realized the reason and the wisdom behind the bishop's reservation. Accordingly, I announced to the staff that we were not going to jeopardize our entire liturgical program and our favorable reputation by allowing a few televised images to publicly confirm what Bishop Begin had aptly labeled our "penchant for anticipating future reforms." No female ministers were assigned to the service. The entire acolyte contingent, male and female, was justifiably outraged. Stoically I took the heat. Two months later — to the world's consternation — Pope John Paul the First died unexpectedly. Lucky for me the media failed to call!

One day, when all of the construction and remodeling required by the closure of the school and the bishop's residency had been completed, I surveyed the entire parish plant. This included the new community center with its vast patios and parking lots, the remodeled rectory with its new rugs and parquet flooring, the cathedral sanctuary and nave totally recarpeted, and lastly, the Bishop Floyd L. Begin Plaza, which expanded the cathedral's entryway into a sprawling courtyard. I realized then that during my short tenure virtually every inch of walking space on the premises got resurfaced!

That realization prompted me to question the spiritual "grounds" upon which we had built the parish and had been treading those past ten years. *Should they also be inspected for wear and tear? Might they have to be replaced as well?*

As if in answer to my musing, I chanced upon a speech delivered by one of the American Church's more inspired bishops at the U.S. Bishops' Annual Convention. It was a provocative challenge to his peers and to every pastor in the country. I shared his insightful message and my reaction to it with my staff. They were impressed and agreed that we should make it the topic of discussion at our parish council's annual "Day Away." Every year the entire leadership of the parish — all eighty task force members and staff — would gather to set goals and strategies for the year ahead.

This is what I had to say at the opening session:

When I became your pastor two and half years ago, I envisioned my role as that of an administrator entrusted with the job of overseeing a program of service to this parish and to the Diocese. I was primarily concerned about strengthening our four priorities, namely, liturgy, school, services to the aging and community organizing. I was content that the staff was doing an efficient job and that the parish council was functioning in an organized and orderly fashion. Calendars, dates, functions and programs were properly coordinated; people were being serviced, and all departments were reporting success.

In other words, I saw myself at the top of a triangle; underneath me was the parish staff, and below them — at the bottom of this neat little church structure — was the community. Then I heard a talk by Bishop Albert Ottenweller of Toledo, Ohio: "You know," he said, "Christ didn't come to build a pyramid. He came to form a circle. The beauty of the Second Vatican Council was to remind us of that." I think the bishop is right! Consequently, I believe we may have to revamp our priorities, our outlook and our agenda. Perhaps we should focus more on forming circles than on stretching out a hand to those "below" us. I invite you to discuss the matter and see whether you agree with Ottenweller's view about Christ's method of dealing with one another and Vatican II's providential recovery of it. If so, how are we going to face the challenge of this new vision? Could we possibly come up with a set of goals and a five-year plan to implement them?"

The result of the group's deliberations was a *Vision Statement* that radically altered our entire priority system. "*In five years [1982],*" it stated, "*St. Francis de Sales parish will be a group of individuals pursuing spiritual growth through Christian community, accepting responsibility for ministry, and attempting to meet the spiritual, physical and educational needs of ourselves and others.*"

Henceforth the main focus of the parish would not be "worship" as such; it would be to foster the *spirituality* of its members through an experience of *community*. Liturgy would continue to be the preeminent source of these objectives, but the vision statement demanded that they pervade as well all our nonliturgical gatherings.

It took us all a while to get used to the change. The finance committee, for example, had to learn to prioritize the budget around activities promoting spiritual growth, such as retreats, days of renewal and adult education. Eventually they agreed to fund costly programs designed to facilitate spiritual bonding through small-group interaction and reflection upon the Scriptures.

The members of the Social Events Task Force had to focus on the spiritual dimension of hospitality when planning parish socials and parties. The acolytes and the ministers of the Eucharist instituted monthly get-togethers in their homes in order to deepen their understanding of their respective ministries. The lectors assigned to read the Scriptures at the weekend liturgies had been getting together every Tuesday night for years. (If a lector failed to attend the Tuesday session, he/she was excluded from reading on Sunday.) Consequently they served as a model for the other groups, who committed themselves to "forming circles." Even the choir was sent away on a yearly retreat to the Napa Valley. The quality and depth of the spiritual experience at these intense weekends transformed the musicians and singers into more committed music ministers and more proficient performers.

Father Joseph M. Champlin, a national author and columnist who had been chronicling the history and developments in Oakland over the years, wrote in *The Church Family*, August 10, 1981 an article entitled "A More Spiritual Approach."

> . . . Externally, it would appear that not much has changed in a dozen years.
>
> But Father Osuna tells me their approach today is on a much deeper, spiritual level.
>
> The entire choir, for example, annually goes away for a weekend retreat at the parish's expense (cost, $2,000). On Saturday morning of this renewal experience, a professor comes from an area university to lecture, not on music, but on spirituality.
>
> Other groups of ministers like ushers, lectors, Eucharistic distributors also have regular days or evenings of prayer and recollection, times for intensifying their lives of prayer.

When I participated in Sunday Mass at the Oakland Cathedral during the late '60's the liturgy seemed very prayerful indeed and in no way a show, entertainment or performance. Nevertheless, Osuna believes this more spiritual approach has deepened the level of faith in both those who serve and those served.

He also senses the musicians currently possess a much clearer awareness of their role as ministers at the altar, people called by God in a unique way to assist others at worship. If, before, these persons played or sang merely because they enjoyed making music with their natural talents, the motivation now is steadier and loftier. Those people grasp better that through birth and baptism they have been summoned to use their divine gifts for a noble purpose.

In 1967 the Church issued an Instruction on Sacred Music. Paragraph 24 gives explicit theoretical support for what the Oakland leaders have been doing in practice:

"Besides musical formation, suitable liturgical and spiritual formation must also be given to the members of the choir, in such a way that the proper performance of their liturgical role will not only enhance the beauty of the celebration and be an excellent example for the faithful, but will bring spiritual benefit to the choir-members themselves."

The second element in the *Vision Statement* highlighted a parishioner's commitment to ministry. The fruit of one's spiritual life should blossom into service within the community. Every member is called to take ownership of some aspect of the parish's day-to-day operation — and be accountable for it. The phrase "Let staff do it!" would no longer hold water. *Responsibility* for parish life rests upon everyone. That included taking the initiative in setting up programs and activities, and the blame if or when they failed.

Gradually this subtle but noticeable emphasis on spirituality within the leadership spread to the people of the parish. Made aware of the vision statement through a series of liturgies, the congregation at large began to respond to and call for a simpler style of worship.

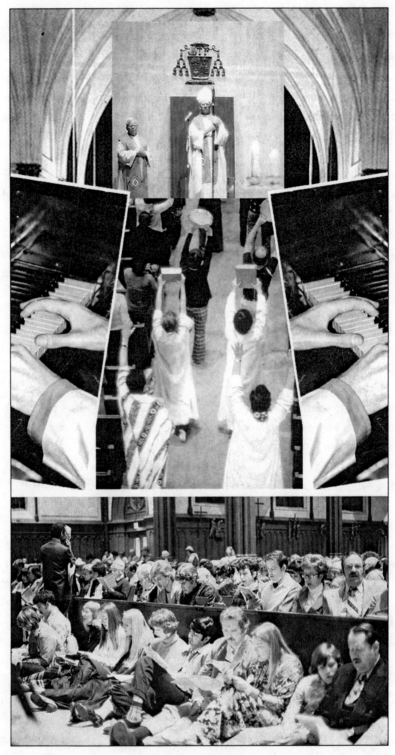

From "Pyramid"

To "Circle"

Chapter Thirteen:

It's a Classic!

A simpler style of worship? Yes, but not in July! Pulling out all "creative stops" once a year was too cherished a tradition to be suppressed! The people of the parish looked forward to it, as did the vacationing groups of religious students who flocked to the Bay Area's colleges and seminaries for summer workshops.

It's a Classic was the title of the 1978 series. Of all our creative efforts, these four liturgies rank among the most artistically challenging, spiritually insightful and liturgically successful. Nick Meyerhoffer, a member of our liturgy committee and a future professor of German Literature at Northern Arizona University, proposed that we explore the world of the *classics*. A book, a play or an opera becomes a classic, he contended, because it expresses artistically a reality that is intrinsically *human,* something universally experienced and spiritually valid for all. As such, he continued, a classic embodies some fundamental tenet of our Christian Tradition and Scriptures, which are the preeminent depositories of all human values. "Why don't we take a look at some of these classics," he asked, "and celebrate the connection?"

After discussing various classical structures and scenarios, the committee adopted the progression originally used by Dante Alighieri in his *Divina Comedia*: "Inferno, Purgatorio, Paradiso."

The first Sunday was to feature the legend of *Faust*, with its perceptive lesson: Academic political and economic pursuits do not provide a definitive answer to the human mind's search for truth and power. Moreover, they inevitably lead to a confrontation with the Devil! The equivalent of Purgatory, it was agreed, is allegorically portrayed in the tale of *Romeo and Juliet*, which tragically confirms that youthful passion is not the heart's ultimate fulfillment; its spells and potions are lethal. For the third Sunday, the committee decided that Dante's own tour of Paradise, with the lovely Beatrice replacing the poet Virgil as guide, would most vividly convey the classic truth that even Beauty and the Arts can never fully satisfy the human soul.

But what can? And where is it expressed in the classic repertory? We all acknowledged that for "Carnival Sunday" we needed to come up with a work that was evangelically profound but playful and upbeat at the same time — "something children can understand." Silence fell over the group as everyone scavenged through their mental catalogue of epics, myths and fables. Then in a flash of inspiration a jubilant voice blurted out: "St. Exupery's *The Little Prince!*"

The Temptation of Faust was the title of the first Sunday's sermon, obligingly delivered by the Devil who introduced himself to the overflowing congregation as the legendary Mephistopheles. His real name was The Reverend Edward C. Hobbs, Episcopal priest and Professor of Theology at Berkeley's Graduate Theological Union. His monologue was preceded by the required Scripture readings, and by the appearance of Dr. Nicolas Meyerhoffer in academic robes, representing Doctor Faustus. Obviously bored with life, the celebrated scholar ambled over to the Bible enthroned on the altar, scornfully flipped through its pages, then wearily seated himself and fell asleep. That's when Satan, also in academic attire, approached the pulpit and began his homily:

> Faust! A wise fool indeed. You are, of course, but a representative of all mankind. You   wish to possess the whole, to feel and recognize the highest as well as the deepest. And through it all you fail to see that such presumption can only lead to eternal dissatisfaction. . . And so, my insatiable one, you will be easy game for me! I, the eternal denier, the perpetual negative, will bring you to the heights that you by nature lack, but they shall not suffice.

You will turn away from the mind and turn to the physical pleasures of life. This, too, will deceive you, since submergence in the lusts and passions of the body will not succeed in satisfying your thirst for the abundance of existence. It will only make you discover, after all, the reality of guilt, the realization that you too cannot exist outside the confines of morality.

Still failing to grasp the meaning of life's play, you will seek to still your longing by addressing yourself to the great, the impossible deed. And your attempt to rule and turn back the sea will indeed succeed! Yet even now I see you in your state of seeming triumph, grown old, but not contented; rich, but not wise; powerful, but not good. There will always be something left for you to wish, always a lack of something to quiet your restless will.

O yes, my dissatisfied titan, with you I shall have my fun!

After masterfully elaborating the theme to its logical conclusion, the persuasive Mephistopheles stepped from the pulpit, approached the awakened Faust, helped him to his feet, and triumphantly escorted him into the darkened sacristy. As the two black-robed professors faded from sight, the choir intoned John Foley's plaintive setting of Isaiah's prophetic text:

> *Turn to me, O turn, and be saved, says the Lord,*
> *for I am God; there is no other, none beside me.*
> *I call your name.* (45:22–23)

The Jesuit priest who agreed to coordinate the second Sunday's liturgy managed to recruit a young Jesuit scholastic for the role of Romeo and a recently ordained Methodist minister as Juliet. Both had been trained in classical ballet. The celebrant of the Mass, of course, was Friar Laurence, the Shakespearean couple's family chaplain. Vested in a Franciscan robe and mediaeval stole, the preacher retold the classic love affair as the graceful couple revealed in exquisite choreography its romantic and tragic unfolding to the accompaniment of Bach's "Air" from *Suite No.3 for Six Strings*. The scripture reading spoke of love as well:

For stern as death is love,
relentless as the nether world is devotion;
its flames are a blazing fire.
Deep waters cannot quench love, nor floods sweep it away.
Were one to offer all he owns to purchase love,
he would be roundly mocked. (Song of Songs 8:6–7*)*

But strong as it is, the homilist commented, youthful passion is self-centered and self-destructive, and can claim to be but a faint reflection of a purer love that surrenders to death in order to redeem and give life.

In this way the love of God was revealed to us:
God sent his only Son into the world
so that we might have life through him.
In this is love, not that we have loved God,
but that he loved us
and sent his Son as expiation for our sins.
Beloved, if God so loved us,
we also must love one another. (I John 4:9–11)

"Now that's a love story!" he concluded.

Father Antonio Valdivia, my close friend and now a popular orator, was selected to preach on *Il Paradiso*. The key to this section of Dante's masterpiece, he insightfully pointed out, was the appearance of the beautiful Beatrice as guide. A male poet had been the ideal escort through Hell and Purgatory, he explained, but the delights of Heaven can only be revealed by a woman. "The Feminine," he asserted, "is the gateway to higher human experience."

To articulate this notion pictorially, Patricia Walsh, our resident artist, combed through the archives of the College of Arts and Crafts (where she taught) for historical renderings of Mary, the mother of Jesus, and assembled them into a four-minute slide presentation. The Maiden-Madonna's image unfolded on the screen in its myriad manifestations throughout the history of Art. In the background, Diane Gilfeather, a beautiful and gifted lyric soprano, sang Schubert's incomparable setting of the *Ave Maria*, ". . . Blessed are you among women . . . ."

The impact was akin to a spiritual meltdown: disarming, touching, tender, captivating, heartwarming, and uplifting — a *tour de force*!

Father Valdivia's homily elaborated the significance of what the assembly had experienced and was feeling: "Anima," he reminded his hearers, "is the Latin word for soul. It is a feminine noun. Follow *her* lead," he counseled, "for *she* is your ticket to transcendence!"

Jack Miffleton's masterful script for the fourth Sunday's climactic liturgy read as follows:

Five Scenes from *The Little Prince.* Resonating Scripture: Matthew 6:19–21; 26–33

> *. . . But seek first the kingdom of God and his righteousness and all these things will be given you besides.* (6:33)

> *CAST:* *   Narrator/Aviator
>   Little Prince
>   King
>   Lamplighter
>   Snake   *puppet operated by Faust or Mephistopheles*
>   Roses+   *spoken for by Shakespeare*
>   Fox+   *puppet operated by Dante*

The Narrator tells of his meeting with the young protagonist and their subsequent parting:

> The Little Prince traveled from his planet in search of the knowledge he needed to understand and love his flower better . . . His travels brought him to many places and finally to Earth where he discovered the secret of what is really important in life. In many ways my encounter with the Little Prince changed my life and today it gives me the courage to share with you a few of the adventures of this Little Prince, some of which grownups may find difficult to understand.

---

* All the roles were performed by Cathedral regulars with exception of the Little Prince, who was recruited from another parish. This was the youngster's first acting experience. It prompted him to choose a career in the musical theater and to fulfill the role of cantor at his local parish.

+ Instead of puppets, these roles were performed by live actors.

The Little Prince began his journey in search of knowledge by visiting neighboring asteroids. He was disappointed with the King and the Lamplighter who seemed completely unenlightened regarding the important things in life. When he arrives on earth he is equally disillusioned by the death-dealing Snake and puzzled by the garden "all abloom with roses." But finally he encounters the Fox who teaches him how to "establish ties," make friends and be responsible for one's love, thus providing him with the secret of what is really important in life.

"It is only with the heart that one sees rightly. What is essential is invisible to the eye. It is the time you wasted for your rose that makes your rose so important . . .Men have forgotten this truth, but you must not forget it. You become responsible, forever, for what you have tamed. You are responsible for your rose."

Bishop Cummins was not present for this particular liturgy. But one of his recent acquaintances was. He sent the bishop the following letter.

Dear Bishop Cummins:

Pursuant to your suggestion at lunch at St. Mary's College last Friday, my wife and I attended the 10:30 liturgy at your Cathedral last Sunday, the celebration featuring the story of the Little Prince. It was a moving and faith-enriching experience for both of us.

Prior to our marriage two years ago, we both had been active in the planning and celebration of the liturgy — myself as a parish priest and Newman Chaplain . . . and my wife as a grade school principal and parish Director of Religious Education. We both agreed that we have never experienced the kind of celebrative liturgy that we did in Oakland last Sunday. For my own part, I did not think such liturgy was possible. I thought it was in the realm of the ideal and, after years of hoping, had come to the conclusion that it was impossible to experience in the concrete — one of those useful myths that one keeps before oneself as a goal to encourage at least some progress forward from the status quo. Imagine my surprise and delight to see it incarnate right there in Oakland!

Beyond the liturgy itself, we got the feeling at the Carnival that there really was a Christian community life that flowed into and out of the liturgy — in other words, that the liturgy was more than a nice theatrical performance. It was a turning point for us to see that this is really a possibility in a parish setting!

Best wishes,
B. N. B.

1978 **It's a Classic** *summer series' concluding liturgy* **The Little Prince**

1978 **It's a Classic** *summer series' concluding liturgy* **The Little Prince**

Chapter Fourteen:

Never an Undramatic Moment

In December of 1977 my mother, Gaudencia, passed away. Her funeral Mass entered the annals of legend because of my brother Jess' memorable liturgical performance. Since he was a professional actor, I naturally asked him to proclaim the New Testament reading, a relatively short passage from the letter of Paul to the Romans. After scanning the two paragraphs, his brow furrowed. "What does it mean?" he asked. I told him to read over the whole epistle and the meaning of the passage would become evident. Like a seasoned artist and student of his trade, he disappeared for several hours, poring over the lines of the message he was to convey to a receptive group of mourners.

He accomplished the assignment with electrifying effect. Never had the words of the Apostle to the Gentiles been delivered with more understanding and conviction. But what made the performance even more dramatic was a "missed cue" that the veteran actor turned to the Lord's advantage. At the conclusion of the scriptural text, my brother paused for a few seconds, strode from the pulpit intending to resume his seat in the front pew. But just as he reached the edge of the sanctuary and was about to descend the steps, he realized his mistake. He had forgotten to conclude the reading with the customary ritual "tag." Snapping his fingers in recognition and wagging his head in self-reproach, he pivoted around, headed back to the pulpit and, in a disarmingly apologetic tone, confessed, "I'm terribly sorry! I forgot the *credits*: This is the Word of the Lord."

The following summer, my brother returned along with my adorable and insightful sister-in-law, Mary Ann "Sidney" Sloan. They came to experience one of our creative liturgies.

On this particular Sunday in our July series, we were examining the myth of *Don Quixote de la Mancha,* that inveterate idealist whose exploits celebrate the seduction and trickery of the illusory.

Lining the sanctuary wall were five large mirrors that reflected back upon the congregation their own image, creating, as it were, the illusion of two congregations. The nave was festooned with banners and tapestries representing the insignia of ancient magi, sorcerers and masters of wizardry. Merlin the Magician in resplendent robes and coned headgear silently accompanied the ministers as they presided over the Eucharist traditionally referred to as "the *Mystery* of Faith."

The fakery of all substitute spiritualities was unmasked, of course, by the Gospel of Jesus of Nazareth who routinely expelled fiends and demons of every kind, and conferred upon his disciples the power to tame the spirits and denizens of the netherworld.

Throughout the entire Mass my brother sat, knelt and stood in his pew with tears streaming down his face, unable to stop crying! I thought to myself, *Boy, have we botched this one!* After Mass I went over to Mary Ann and asked, "What's the matter with Jess? Was the Mass that bad?"

She asked back, "Don't you know what you did to him?"

"No," I replied, hoping for an explanation.

"What did you expect?" said the former actress and producer. "Here is a man whose whole life is the theater. He walks into church one Sunday, and what does he find? All the trappings of his profession: props, costumes, lighting, a script and a sanctuary full of actors! Don, don't you realize what that is saying to him? It is saying: 'What you do for a living is a *holy* thing!'"

As an afterthought, she added, "Wouldn't it be a gift if everyone who came to Mass received the same confirmation?"

Chapter Fifteen:

Memorable Encounters

In January of 1979 I accompanied Bishop Cummins to Mexico, where the recently elected Pope, John Paul II, was inaugurating the first of his many journeys abroad. As a result of our encounter with the new Bishop of Rome, the Cathedral community was enriched with a new song, and the generosity of our rectory chef was historically acknowledged.

The Polish priests of the Diocese asked me if I would take to their honored compatriot "a small token of our felicitation, solidarity and esteem." It was a handsome stole specially designed and fashioned by the Polish community of the Bay Area. "It would be a pleasure," I assured them.

I was wrapping the gift in the rectory kitchen when our Hungarian cook, Judy Lavar, arrived. She asked what I was doing. When she learned of my mission on behalf of the Poles, she offered to help with the wrapping. "Of course," she added, "you must allow me to include a personal memento of my own. Even though I am not 'Ca-to-lique,' I do share one thing in common with the new Papa." After disappearing for a few minutes, she returned with an object bound in a sheet of insulated plastic, which she placed on top of the stole along with a highly scented sealed envelope. Smiling wryly, she secured the parcel with ribbon, garnishing it with a spectacular yellow-and-white bow.

I dutifully lugged the bundle around Guadalajara for two days, hoping for an opportunity to hand it personally to its intended recipient. Late Saturday evening, just hours before the Pope's scheduled departure, we found ourselves jammed into the courtyard of the archdiocesan major seminary amid a sea of students, guests and gate-crashers. Unable to get anywhere close to the main action, we stationed ourselves — fortuitously — next to the "pope-mobile," figuring that the Pontiff would have to board it for his ride to the airport.

We stood there, guarding our post and enjoying the program prepared by the seminarians who enthusiastically serenaded the Pope with a medley of popular canticles. The Pontiff listened with obvious delight to the chorus of a thousand future priests. But when the youthful choir intoned the song "Pescador de Hombres" by the gifted Spaniard Cesareo Gabarain, the Pope flailed his arms in the air and halted the music. "This is my favorite hymn," he announced, "I want to sing it with you but I don't know the words in your language. I will join you in Polish!" Everyone cheered and started the piece over again. Not knowing the words myself, I determined there and then to translate the song into English so that our community back home could sing the new Pope's favorite anthem.

Finally . . . the Supreme Pontiff makes his way over to the customized van that serves as our mainstay and hopeful meeting place. He climbs into the vehicle, smiling and blessing everything in sight. I stare at the white-robed titan immediately above my head, a veritable mountain of charisma radiating the glowing charm and magnetism possessed only by superstars. Then, in one of his panoramic scans of the ocean of faces below him, he sees me! He looks at *me*!

With a glance you embraced me! the chorus keeps saying.

Dexterously, he bends over the railing and, with a personal smile, scoops up the package from my outstretched hands. "*Gracias,*" he whispers. I could have sworn I heard him add: "*Good friend!*"

Not a month after our return from that memorable encounter, Judy, our Hungarian cook, announced that she had received a personal card from *il Papa*.

"What did it say?" I asked in disbelief.

"It said 'Thank you for your kind note and gift.'"

"Well, what did you say in your note?" I asked.

"I simply wrote: 'From one refugee to another.'"

"And what was it that you sent him?" I pressed.

With consummate aplomb, she responded, "What else? A pint of vodka!"

Pescador de Hombres

Here, at the edge of the sea, notwithstanding the wise and the wealthy,
 You came to summon for me to follow.
O Lord, with a glance you embraced me, then you smiled and whispered
 my name.
I've abandoned my boat in the harbor; close to you I will seek other
 shores.

Here in this vessel I own there's no treasure, no weapon of war —
Just gear for fishing and years of toil.
O Lord, with a glance you embraced me, then you smiled and whispered
 my name.
I've abandoned my boat in the harbor; close to you I will seek other
 shores.

Here are the arms you require, tired branches to shelter the wearied,
A love that's striving to grow and blossom.
O Lord, with a glance you embraced me, then you smiled and whispered
 my name.
I've abandoned my boat in the harbor; close to you I will seek other
 shores.

Hear, all you souls that are waiting, hear him saying "Good friend,
 follow me,
The Lord and Fisher from an alien sea."
O Lord, with a glance you embraced me, then you smiled and whispered
 my name.
I've abandoned my boat in the harbor; close to you I will seek other
 shores.

©1980, English translation by E.D.Osuna. Original melody and text ©1979 by Cesareo Gabarain

Normally, I did not have to leave the country in order to meet notable personalities; they came to Oakland. It was always a surprise to find sitting in the Sunday congregation one or other liturgical composer whose music would in time become part of our present-day "classical repertory." I remember getting a call from John Foley, S.J., one of the St. Louis Jesuits who at the time were studying in Berkeley. He told me that he and four seminary classmates were about to launch a new album of songs, entitled *Neither Silver nor Gold*. Would I be willing to preview the collection and possibly perform them at our liturgies? Today the St. Louis Jesuits are called "fathers of contemporary liturgical music." The release of that initial album was the beginning of an avalanche of popular songs that are now standard repertoire in Catholic hymnals: "Be Not Afraid"; "In Earthen Vessels"; "Here I Am, Lord"; "Glory and Praise"; "The Cry of the Poor"; "One Bread, One Body"; "Turn to Me"; "Like a Shepherd" — an endless litany of hits.

One Sunday, someone whispered in my ear, "Lucien Deiss is in the second pew!" I confess I suffered a slight panic attack. Father Lucien Deiss, CSSp, was a well-known French liturgical pioneer and musician whose *Biblical Hymns and Psalms* was "the first significant way that millions of Catholics in the U.S. came to sing the Word of God and treasure it in their hearts." It so happened that I had adapted [plagiarized, appropriated with changes?] one of Father Deiss' short compositions into what became the "Cathedral Great Amen," a staple of every Mass and the climactic conclusion of every Eucharistic Prayer. I was told later that the eminent composer was so impressed with the entire worship experience that he failed to recognize the "theft"!

Father Michael Joncas, who wrote, among many others, the iconic hymn "On Eagle's Wings" (sung at probably every Catholic funeral), spent a few days with us in Oakland before he rose to iconic status himself. Not only did he dazzle the liturgists and musicians of the diocese with his insight and talent at the annual liturgical conference, but graced the cathedral congregation as well with his personal charm and musical artistry. Today, Father Michael Joncas and his work are known worldwide.

The stream of celebrity visitors was continuous; some came at our invitation, others on their own. One Sunday I would be informed that Joe Wise, Carey Landry, Bob Fabing, Bob Hurd or some other composer was in the audience; or that the popular liturgist John Gallen, S.J. was in attendance; or that Cardinal Suenens from Belgium was sitting *incognito* among the laity. It became so intimidating that I gave instructions I was not to be informed who was worshipping with us that day. Among those we invited were extraordinary theologians, scholars and hierarchs: Raymond Brown, S.S.; John Coleman, S.J.; Bishop Kenneth Untner from Saginaw, Michigan; Cardinal Timothy Manning of Los Angeles. For several summers, the liturgical choreographer Carolyn Deitering led workshops and performed interpretive gospel stories, as did members of the drama department from Santa Clara University.

During the 1970s especially, when the American church was looking for ways of implementing the unfolding liturgical changes, more and more individuals came to Oakland in search of inspiration. St. Francis de Sales Cathedral became a magnet attracting the curious and providing new approaches to the creative. The challenge was adapting liturgy to local culture. One notable example was Father George DeCosta, a friend and fellow student from seminary days. This native Islander had been recently assigned to a small parish on the Big Island of Hawaii.

"Don, they're sending me to Malia O Kalani to close it down," he complained. "Even though there are few parishioners," he confessed, "I don't really want to do that. What's your advice?" I told him that when I arrived at St. Francis the congregation was not only small but demoralized as well. I suggested that he try and do what we did: tailor the worship services to the character and personality of those who came to pray. If a spirited and creative liturgical program did not build up the community, then the parish would fall apart on its own.

Father George went back to his little church in Hilo and within a year had a thriving parish. The secret was his creative liturgies that featured all the color, costume and music of Hawaiian heritage and custom. So successful was the revival at Malia that it soon attracted the curiosity and attention of all the Islands, providing Polynesia with a model of what is now called "enculturation."

Finally, in June 1984, the Vatican paid us a visit. It was in the person, no less, of Archbishop Virgilio Noe, Master of Pontifical Liturgical Celebrations and Secretary of the Congregation for Divine Worship and the Discipline of the Sacraments. Fortunately, he came at the invitation of our own Bishop Cummins, who at the time was chairman of the U.S. Bishops' Committee on the Liturgy. (He claims he had been elected to that prestigious office because of the cathedral's national notoriety.)

The archbishop and future cardinal, whose familiar figure flanked that of Pope John Paul II on all his televised liturgies, was accompanied by an unknown Benedictine monk from the Isle of Wight whose name was Dom Cuthbert Johnson, OSB, and whose role was that of secretary to the Secretary. It was this young, diminutive cleric who, late that first evening, after his boss had retired, exposed the following information in a dramatic, staccato British brogue:

"You know, Father Osuna, that in Rome we have an enormous file on the Oakland Cathedral." He illustrated the size of the file by extending his scrawny arms to their full length. "At the last meeting of the Congregation for Divine Worship," he continued, "it was mentioned that the Oakland Cathedral has been called a 'Mecca of liturgy . . .'" Then, in a solemn aside, he stage-whispered, ". . . to the immense consternation of the Cardinals present." Suddenly he lifted his small frame to its full stature — which was not very tall — and trumpeted, "It was I, I'll have you know, my dear Father Osuna, it was I who had to clarify for Their Eminences the reality of the situation. 'No, no,' I interjected, 'there is no need for concern or censure. I can assure Your Eminences that at Oakland Cathedral the sacred liturgies are *not* conducted in Arabic!'"

After a polite round of tittering, we all retired.

The next day was Pentecost, the feast of the conferral of the Holy Spirit upon the apostles. On the first Pentecost the primitive Church, revived and emboldened by divine energy and fire, burst forth into the public arena to proclaim to an assembly of people from around the world the Gospel of the Risen Lord. The biblical account from the Acts of the Apostles (2:10) relates that among the throng were "travelers from Rome." Bishop Cummins mentioned this in his homily at the 10:30 a.m. Mass at which he presided and Archbishop Noe concelebrated. He also hoped that our Vatican emissary would take back with him a favorable experience of the renewed liturgy as practiced in the United States.

That turned out to be an understatement. Noe and his entourage were ecstatic! The liturgy unfolded flawlessly and was performed with our customary communal enthusiasm, musical and artistic excellence and prayerful bravado. For our people, it was just another "creative celebration," but for our Vatican guests it was an epiphany. One could feel the presence of the Holy Spirit putting a stamp of approval on one community's efforts to infuse and enflesh with soul and vitality the Vatican Council's liturgical reforms.

After the liturgy, the Secretary of the Congregation for Divine Worship remarked, "That was transcendent!" Judging from the smile on his beaming face and the bounce in his casual gait, one would suspect that the Papal Master of Ceremonies had experienced something unusually liberating. Could it be that the learned liturgist from Rome had picked up some new ideas in California?

One must credit Bishop Cummins for sensing that Rome may have had an inaccurate appraisal of the liturgical reform in the United States in general and of his cathedral in particular. His effort to allow members of the Congregation to experience firsthand a liturgy in Oakland and interact with liturgists in the States would provide the Roman authorities with a clearer picture. Perhaps, as a result of this trip, positive feedback based on personally corroborated evidence might find its way into those "enormous files" supervised by Dom Cuthbert.

It was Bishop Cummins' hope that Noe's visit would lead to a fuller understanding of and a more open-minded disposition toward the American liturgical experiment. For a time, at least, it did.

Liturgical choreographer Carolyn Deitering with workshop participants

Bishop John S. Cummins; bottom: flanked by the Vatican's Archbishop
Virgilio Noe (left) and Dom Cuthbert Johnson, OSB (right)

Chapter Sixteen:

A Pipe Organ at Last!

The decade of the seventies that witnessed the resignation of Richard Nixon and the underwhelming administration of Gerald Ford continued to unravel at a sorry pace as the Iranian hostage crisis dismantled Jimmy Carter's promising presidency and boosted the ultraconservative Ronald Reagan into the White House. In Britain, Margaret Thatcher and her Tory party embarked upon an aggressive political course that would eventually lead to war in the South Atlantic. And Pope John Paul II, basking in the applause and limelight of a global stage, began to forge a calculated effort to corral and control the ecclesiastic pluralism unleashed by the Second Vatican Council. Sensing the changing tide, citizen and churchgoer alike started to realign their political postures, with the more liberal among them recoiling into protective silence while the "silent majority" began to clear their liberated vocal cords.

Affected no doubt by this backward slide toward the "traditional," I convinced myself that the time had come for St. Francis to get its long-awaited pipe organ. It was the one musical element that had been forsaken and so long overdue. What's more, I felt that it was essential in order to enhance the quality and depth of our liturgies, which were assuming a more prayerful focus. Moreover, as "blenders of every genre of music," it was imperative that we add to our repertoire of sacred sound the majestic voice of the "king of instruments."

There was another reason: Any cathedral without a pipe organ is simply incomplete —like an opera house without an orchestra. People who worship at the bishop's church deserve to have their prayer appropriately accompanied by the Church's traditional instrument. Lastly, there was no excuse for postponing any longer Bishop Begin's original plan for creating a "model of Vatican II liturgy," which by definition included a musical instrument of exceptional quality to match the other architectural elements.

But would I be able to convince the finance committee and the parish council? The projected cost was $125,000 (the current price tag for the same instrument that ten years ago cost $35,000). How was I to get their authorization? What to do?

Then one day Father David McCarthy, our newly ordained associate pastor, informed me that some friends of his wanted to make a donation to a "worthy cause." Would I meet with them and suggest some options? Not really knowing what the well-groomed couple from Southern California had in mind or how much they intended to contribute, I outlined our parish priorities and some specific programs in need of funding: Sister Maureen's outreach to the neighborhood, the Education Task Force's plans for an expanded youth program, and finally my own personal "dream" of purchasing a new pipe organ to round out our liturgical and musical goals.

After deliberating for a few days, Donald and Darlene Shiley returned to personally announce their decision. It was their desire to be the first contributors to the New Organ Fund with an initial grant of $25,000!

My next move was to approach Father Bill Macchi, the diocesan financial secretary, regarding the feasibility of underwriting the project. Of course, I guaranteed that the entire cost would be covered by the private donations I intended to raise. To my delight, he agreed. He furthermore acceded to my request to set up a special account — separate from the parish's general fund — to expedite all financial transactions relating to the construction and installation of the new instrument.

Armed with a substantial grant and a creditable sponsor, I braced myself for the hard part: getting the parish Executive Committee to approve the proposal. The sixteen members of the Cathedral's policy and decision-making body took very seriously their mandate of running a high-profile operation with relatively little income. In order for them to give their blessing to such a major undertaking I would have to do two things: persuade them of the importance of the project, and secondly, convince them that it would not cost the parish a single penny.

First I obtained the unanimous support of the finance committee and secured a written endorsement from its chairman; then I made a formal presentation to the full Executive Committee in the fall of 1979, two months before leaving on a scheduled sabbatical. (If I got the green light I would spend much of my free time overseeing the details of the organ project and raising the needed cash.) A few members objected to the proposal, but the majority of the committee voted in favor of "allowing the pastor to arrange for the future installation of a pipe organ" according to certain stipulated conditions. In order to forestall any future misunderstanding, I asked that the committee's discussion and the results of the voting be duly recorded and entered into the minutes. And it was a good thing I did, because three years later the issue came back to haunt us!

The contract for the two-manual twenty-nine-rank pipe organ was awarded to the San Francisco firm of Schoenstein and Company. Its external artistic design was the creation of Lawrence Schoenstein, the last surviving member of the renowned family of organ builders. His asymmetrical arrangement of long fluted pipes ascending and descending in dramatic sweeps, from the floor of the choir area to the massive stained-glass window high in the north transept, was breathtaking. The organ's internal specifications (an array of stops and combinations) were the product of a stellar group of Bay Area organists whose expertise and experience resulted in an instrument of enormous versatility.

As I promised the parish council, I began to solicit funds for the new musical addition from several local Catholic philanthropists. One wealthy patron who granted me an interview greeted me with the candid statement: "I don't know much about organs, but I do know a bit about Lear jets." Then he opened a desk drawer and pulled out an illustrated catalogue of various models of aircraft. "Can you tell the difference," he asked, "between this plane and this one?" (They looked the same to me.) "Well, this one costs half a million dollars and the other one twice as much. On the outside they look the same, but on the inside one is fitted with the latest state-of-the-art equipment. That accounts for the difference in price." Then, leaning forward, he asked intently:

"Now, what kind of an organ do you intend to buy?"

I had to think about the import of the question for a second. Then I replied:

"Probably something like a well-equipped Cessna!"

"Well then," he chuckled, "you'll be hearing from me!"

No sooner had the imposing instrument been installed and dedicated in 1982 when a few parish council members, including some who voted for the motion, began to grumble and complain: "The money should have been spent on the poor!" An undercurrent of negativity and ill will began to pervade the rest of the leadership and threatened to spread through the entire community. After analyzing the nature and origin of the dissension, I concluded that a far more subtle and insidious issue lay at the heart of the malaise.

With the consent and support of the staff, I obtained the services of a professional psychologist trained in "facilitation and mediation" and asked the council chairman to call a special meeting of the Executive Committee. From this one confrontation I gleaned a valuable lesson regarding (1) the dynamics of authority, (2) the real nature of leadership, and (3) the effectiveness of open and forthright dialogue in resolving disputes.

The session was held in the comfortable home of one of our staff. The facilitator began by asking each participant to share his or her concept of the "problem." As we went around the room listening to each member's assessment and apprehension, I concluded that my analysis had been right on target. The facilitator suggested that I be the last to speak.

"From what most of you have shared," I began, "the real problem doesn't seem to be with the new organ. What's bothering many of you is that the organ has come to symbolize a deeper uneasiness. A conflict regarding parish policy and political power has developed between the parish leadership and the pastor!"

Stunned silence; heads lower; limbs twitch…

"You obviously feel," I continued, "that the pastor, by promoting and successfully accomplishing a 'pet project,' has overstepped his role and willfully bypassed the lawful authority of the parish council. And what's more, judging from what you have said, some of you are afraid that unless he's checked he will do it again!"

I could tell by the squirming that I was on the right track.

"So now," I summarized, "the 'problem' is not about the merits of a musical instrument; it's about the moral orthodoxy of the pastor!"

This remark seemed to ease the tension in the room, as smiles appeared and bodies rearranged themselves comfortably. I began to feel a sense of support and validation. But I was not finished.

"Isn't it a fact," I reminded the group, "that I asked for and received permission from the committee to undertake the project in the first place? The official minutes of the meeting confirm that. The vote could have just as easily gone against granting permission, could it not? Now, does that sound like circumvention of authority?"

Any remaining hostility drained from the faces that now looked intently into mine.

"You are the leaders of the parish," I continued, "so let me say a few words about leadership. In the beginning, before there was a parish council, who was it that transformed our demoralized community into a vibrant parish family? And who was it — when the time was right — that entrusted the running of the parish over to you? It was our pastors, wasn't it? You rightfully looked to them for guidance, for inspiration; you expected them to lead, to challenge and point to new horizons.

"Then why is it," I asked in conclusion, "that some of you suspect that this pastor was looking for ways to get around or override the very structure that he helped create and nourish? Does the gift of a one-hundred-twenty-five-thousand -dollar pipe organ constitute a political power-play? Or might it be my way of pointing us all toward a higher liturgical and cultural horizon? I challenge you to show as much energy and enterprise in coming up with projects that will improve our service to the community if you think they are important enough to pursue. You will find that if your dreams resonate with the needs of the people, you will be successful. So now let's get back to working with one another in a spirit of mutual trust and respect!"

We concluded the session with a brief prayer of thanksgiving and shared with one another the Kiss of Peace. Euphoria set in as we hugged and smiled and breathed sighs of relief. All vestiges of resentment dissipated as we basked in the glow of a recovered relationship.

The professional facilitator beamed and drawled, "You Catholics sure know how to 'kiss and make up.'"

To add to the great joy and fortune of all, Mario Balestrieri was hired as cathedral organist. This young, enormously gifted San Franciscan, with a fresh master's degree in organ performance from San Francisco State University, undertook his appointment with enthusiasm, artistry and geniality. As accompanist to choir and congregation, as well as concert performer, "Maestro Mario B" increasingly enhanced our prayer with a new, invigorating and majestic sonority.

The Oakland Cathedral's Shoenstein Organ, installed 1982

Cathedral Organist, Mario Balestrieri

Chapter Seventeen:

Hidden Treasure

Originally, I had told myself that I was never going to become a pastor: It wouldn't suit my personality or my gifts. But the rectorship of the Cathedral was an assignment I could hardly have refused. When I accepted, however, I promised myself to keep the job for ten years only. After five years, I decided to request a year's sabbatical in order to take stock and recharge the soul. Besides, my little dog, Muffin, was getting a bit too tense and testy from all the pressure!

So in the fall of 1980 both of us headed off to St. Patrick's Seminary in Menlo Park for a few months of rest and study. We settled on my old *alma mater* because of the expansive grounds and spacious lawns where Muffin could roam freely and hunt for elusive gophers. For my part, the place offered a library, stimulating companions, three meals a day, and an easy hour-and-a-half ride to the Oakland Cathedral to which we returned every weekend to lead the worship services.

I entrusted the day-to-day administration of the parish to our newly appointed associate pastor, P. Michael Galvan, one of the few Native Americans ever to be ordained a Catholic priest. I felt confident that the young "warrior" would benefit from some hands-on experience before becoming a pastoral "chief." His most challenging assignment was to oversee the repainting of the exterior of the cathedral church and bell tower. I wasn't particularly worried because, since the Diocese had agreed to pick up the $70,000 tab, I figured that Chancery officials would be carefully monitoring the expensive enterprise.

But, to my astonishment, I came home one weekend to find the formerly "bone white" cathedral aglow in a fresh coat of ivory paint with a distinct tinge of mustard! Asked for an explanation, Father Michael responded that his instructions were to "paint the church 'off white.'" From the various samples of off-white shown him by the painters he had merely selected the one with the name that most appealed to him: "Apache Muslin!" When the negligent diocesan officials saw the results, their faces turned off-white with a tinge of red!

Despite the mild mishap, it was a tribute to the staff and council that the parish could function smoothly enough without the pastor having to be on site all the time. The fact that I checked in at the end of every week provided a degree of continuity and support. I also brought with me the fruits of my sabbatical creativity: new musical arrangements for the choir and ensemble, and for the congregation a new setting of various parts of the Mass which I dedicated to my mother and which bore her name: *Missa Gaudencia*.

A good bit of my sabbatical year was spent in the seminary library researching the history and development of the Roman Rite. From past studies I knew that the rites and rituals of the Church had undergone numerous changes and adaptations over the centuries. But I had not realized the role that artistic and cultural creativity had played in the evolutionary process. To my surprise, I discovered that the rituals celebrated throughout the Christian world were originally the products of individuals or communities who blended social, geographical and cultural elements with local devotional practices to produce inspired expressions of faith — much like the authors of the Scriptures had done in composing the books of the Bible.

Clearly, the history of the Roman Rite was a continuous series of adaptations, modifications and even blendings of ceremonies from diverse traditions. This fluid process continued until the reforms of the Council of Trent (1545–63), which issued a new rite for the universal Church that bore its name: Tridentine. It remained virtually unchanged for four centuries. Then in 1962 the Second Vatican Council mandated that the Tridentine rituals be revised "in light of sound tradition, and that they be given new vigor to meet the circumstances and needs of modern times." (*Constitution on the Sacred Liturgy,* para. 4)

This latest example of the regenerative evolution of Catholic worship had the effect of reinstating a certain "pluralism" to the Church's ceremonials. It allowed optional alternatives and provided flexibility to the stylized rituals of the immediate past, thus harkening back to the practice of more ancient times. Vatican II reforms also permitted national conferences of bishops to promote liturgical customs that represent more closely the cultural heritage of particular regions. Under the banner of "enculturation," the Council called for freshness and a vitality to permeate the worship and prayer of the People of God from East and West.

Meaningful contemporary rituals, like those of the past, will surface only after a period of creative experimentation. Controversy inevitably ensues, but as one U. S. bishop recently stated:

> You have to look at it over a great historical sweep. Sometimes, you know, the church discovers that through the activities of persons whose views don't carry the day at a given time — that they were planting the seeds of the things that the church gradually adopted and made its own. (Bishop Matthew H. Clark, Rochester, NY, 1998)

One welcome reform was the publication of a new lectionary for Sundays in which the readings from the Old and New Testaments were spread over three years: Cycle A, Cycle B and Cycle C. (Prior to this, only one set of readings was used year after year.) This expanded collection of passages from the Bible gave Sunday worshipers a wider exposure to and a deeper appreciation of the Word of God. It also provided our Liturgy Task Force with a broader palette of themes and topics to meditate upon and attempt to enhance and reinforce with fresh and creative touches.

A good example is the Cycle A Gospel readings for the four Sundays of July 1981 featuring Chapter 13 of Matthew's Gospel, in which Christ describes the kingdom of heaven in seven imaginative parables. It made for a memorable summer series that was called *Hidden Treasure.*

The first Sunday featured the parable about the sower whose seed landed on different kinds of surfaces: a path, rocky ground, shallow soil, among thorns, and finally upon rich earth. The disciples asked Jesus, "Why do you speak to them in parables?"

Quoting Isaiah, the Lord answered, "This is why I speak to them in parables, because 'they look but do not see and hear but do not listen or understand.'"

This enigmatic answer caused the liturgy committee to think long and hard as to what Jesus meant. Once we had figured it out, we looked for appropriate "channels" to convey the power and depth of Christ's response.

We did not have to look very far. Tony lived in a nearby senior residence. He was a man whom everyone loved and enjoyed, not just because he serenaded the neighborhood with his accordion and Italian arias, but because he radiated an inner joy and exuberance that bespoke a loving and giving spirit. Tony was blind.

Coincidentally, that summer, a liturgical performance troupe from Santa Clara University in San Jose, California, volunteered to collaborate with us in one of our summer series. One of its members was a visiting college student from England who was a remarkably gifted dancer despite a physical handicap that rendered him unable to hear or speak.

And so, for our first "Hidden Treasure" the congregation was introduced to Tony who read from a Bible in Braille, and to our nonspeaking, nonhearing visitor from across the Atlantic who proclaimed the second reading in silence — using only the language of his body.

I can still see the congregation's stunned reaction as our smiling accordion player, cane in hand, makes his way up the sanctuary steps, groping with outstretched arms for the pulpit. Once there, he balances his shoulders, steadies his legs and places both hands on the Bible before him. Squaring his chin over the audience, he focuses on an imaginary listener and begins to speak the text which his fingers informs him is from the prophet Isaiah. In melodious staccato phrases, he gives voice to — and for the moment becomes the embodiment of — the Old Testament visionary himself:

> Just as from the heavens the rain and snow come down
> and do not return there till they have watered the earth,
> making it fertile and fruitful,
> giving seed to him who sows and bread to him who eats,
> so shall my word be that goes forth from my mouth;

> it shall not return to me void, but shall do my will,
> achieving the end for which I sent it. (Isaiah 55:10–11)

The effect was electrifying. People sat in shock as the meaning of the prophecy silently reverberated around the frame of the aged lector hobbling to a chair next to the main celebrant. But it was a minor sensation compared to the sobering jolt that stunned the assembly when the handsome British student approached center stage and began proclaiming in silent, graphic choreography a passage from the letter of Paul to the Romans — one that he had obviously understood and made his own even though his ears had never registered the words nor his tongue articulated its consoling message:

> I consider the sufferings of the present to be as nothing compared with the glory to be revealed in us . . . Yes, we know that all creation groans and is in agony even until now. Not only that, but we ourselves, although we have the Spirit as first fruits, groan inwardly while we await the redemption of our bodies. (8:18–23)

When he had finished, the dancer sat down next to the celebrant flanked now on the one side by a blind man and on the other by a deaf-mute. Addressing the two of them as if they were the only ones in church, Father Michael announced the proclamation of the Gospel reciting from memory the (formerly enigmatic) words of Jesus:

> I use parables when I speak to them *[pointing to the congregation]*
> because they look but do not see,
> they listen but do not hear or understand . . .
>
> *[turning to Tony]*
> But blessed are your eyes, because they see,
> *[then to the English student]*
> and your ears, because they hear.
>
> Amen, I say to you, many prophets and righteous people
> longed to see what you see but did not see it,
> and hear what you hear and did not hear it.
>
> *[addressing the assembly]*

Hear, then, the parable of the sower . . . .

The subsequent liturgies in the series dealt with the other six parables that compared the kingdom of heaven to a mustard seed that grew into the "largest of plants"; and to a bit of yeast that leavened a large mound of dough; a treasure buried in a field and a pearl of great price, which those who found them purchased after selling all they possessed. These images focus on the kingdom as a reality that at first is small but which grows in volume and value as it is nurtured and appreciated.

The remaining two parables describe the kingdom as a haven for all: the weeds (darnel) among the wheat, and the "net thrown into the sea which collects fish of every kind. When it is full they haul it ashore and sit down to put what is good into buckets. What is bad they throw away."

It was this last image of the dragnet that helped us celebrate on "Carnival Sunday" our identity as seekers and subjects of the kingdom who, having been dragged together by the grace of Christ, were privileged to enjoy the diversity and inclusiveness of the Kingdom of Heaven in a run-down section of an inner city in California.

Chapter 13 of Matthew's Gospel concludes with a question and a job description that we at the Oakland Cathedral were committed to respond to and fulfill with the same enthusiasm and resolve as that of the original disciples of Jesus:

"Do you understand all these things?"

They answered, "Yes."

And he replied, "Then every scribe who has been instructed in the kingdom of heaven is like the head of a household who brings from his storeroom both the new and the old." (Matthew 13:51–52).

*1981 **Hidden Treasure**: kingdom parables, Mt 13: "The kingdom is like a net...that collects all kinds..." "Blessed are your eyes...and your ears..."*

Epilogue

Throughout the 1980s, we continued to bring from our storeroom "both the new and the old," aided by the gifted Capuchin liturgist William "Bill" Cieslak, OFM Cap, president of the Franciscan School of Theology in Berkeley. His expertise, enthusiasm and ingenuity provided the cathedral community with inspired worship services year after year.

Especially memorable were the imaginative variations of the solemn rites of Holy Week. Enormous energy, creativity and expense went into making these celebrations the most impressive of the entire year. Palm Sunday featured elaborate processions and jubilant fanfares proclaiming Christ's triumphant entry into Jerusalem; this was followed by a dramatic setting of Christ's passion and death, with lectors performing the roles of narrator, disciples, religious leaders, Pontius Pilate, and so forth. On Holy Thursday a more intimate feeling prevailed as Bishop Cummins washed the feet of individuals in the assembly and those engaged in parish ministries; these in turn renewed their commitment of service to the community. Good Friday's focus was on the mystery of human suffering and emotional trauma that resonates in St. John's account of Christ's passion and death, and in the touching ritual of the Veneration of the Cross.

The solemn Vigil on Holy Saturday night continued to be the most innovative and artistically inventive liturgy of the year — in the tradition of my master's degree thesis (Chapter VIII). Multimedia presentations incorporating a variety of art forms elucidated Scripture passages and retold the history of salvation. The lighting of the Easter fire and the rituals surrounding the Paschal Candle dramatized the rising of Christ from the grave.

The high point of the evening, however, was the initiation of new members into our Catholic community through the ceremony of Profession of Faith and the sacraments of Baptism, Confirmation and Eucharist.

These yearly Lenten-Easter events inspired artists to create masterpieces of resplendent interior design and stimulated choir and musicians to perform works of astounding beauty. All, so that the assembly of worshipers could experience and celebrate the reality of springtime and the end to the ravages of winter.

Year after year, this season of death and renewal memorialized an inner truth about the nature and history of the Oakland Cathedral community itself. Within the short span of twenty-plus years, the dying-rising pattern that unfolded every Holy Week was mirrored in the two decades that witnessed the tragic dismantling of an old parish church that miraculously blossomed into a renovated cathedral, the rise to national recognition and the descent into scandal and disarray; and finally the painstaking rebuilding of a chastened people into an even stronger community of faith and service.

The cycle ended on October 17, 1989 when a magnitude 7.1 earthquake devastated the San Francisco Bay Area — including central Oakland. After inspecting the battered structure at 21st and Grove Streets, authorities forbade anyone from entering St. Francis de Sales Cathedral. The prohibition was never lifted. From that fatal Tuesday onward, no liturgy was ever again celebrated in its hallowed precincts. The worshipers, bereft of their temple and stripped of their familiar gathering place, dispersed. After fruitless efforts at preservation, the crippled structure was razed.

But the phenomenon that was the Oakland Cathedral lives on in the hearts of those whose souls were shaped and enriched by its brief appearance on the stage of history. They cannot forget nor can they fail to appreciate the Oakland Cathedral's principal contribution: a commitment to the vision of the Second Vatican Council and a twenty-one-year effort to steadfastly implement its reforms, especially the sacred liturgy, which, the Council declared, is the "source and summit" of Christian spirituality.

This is the legacy of the Oakland Cathedral: to have provided countless people with an experience of Church so precious and cherished that it would never be forgotten; a memory of worship services that thoroughly nourished the soul every weekend; the memory of belonging to a group of people, including strangers, who were instantly pulled together in a bond of love and acceptance; the memory of participating on an equal basis with the clergy in the everyday work of the Church; a memory that validated the U.S. bishops' statement, "Good liturgy fosters faith,"

To me, those two decades seem like a dream — not unlike Jacob's at the shrine of Bethel:

Then he had a dream: a stairway rested on the ground, with its top reaching to the heavens; and God's messengers were going up and down on it. And there was the Lord standing beside him and saying: "I, the Lord, am the God of your forefather Abraham and the God of Isaac; the land on which you are lying I will give to you and your descendants. These shall be as plentiful as the dust of the earth, and through them you shall spread out east and west, north and south. In you and your descendants all the nations of the earth shall find blessing. Know that I will protect you wherever you go, and bring you back to this land. I will never leave you until I have done what I promised you.

When Jacob awoke from his sleep he exclaimed: "Truly the Lord is in this spot although I did not know it!" In solemn wonder he cried out: "How awesome is this place! This is the gateway to heaven!" (Genesis 28:12–17)

THE END

Celebrating the Paschal Mystery: dying and rising with Christ
Photography by Jerry A. Rubino

Addendum:

New liturgy gives life to old parish

By Mary Ellen Leary

Special to the National
Catholic Reporter

Volume 9 Number 26,
April 27, 1973

OAKLAND, Calif. --- "We set out to create community. But we went about it in a novel way. We decided to focus on a vital, prayerful liturgy and let community grow out of that. We weren't sure it would work. But we thought if we were good enough, it might."

They were good enough.

Each Sunday attests to a spiritual vitality in the Cathedral of St. Francis de Sales on San Francisco Bay's East shore.

The church gained unexpected importance in its old age, when in 1962 it was designated the cathedral for the newly formed Oakland diocese. A remodeled late 19th century edifice, its red brick has been modernized with an over glaze of white, its cluttery angels and saints inside replaced by handsome simplicity of line, dark oak reredos, cream-white walls and rich, golden carpet. Its spire thrusts up from an impoverished skid row setting at the ugly ghetto edge of Oakland's downtown.

In this unlikely neighborhood, two Masses each Sunday, 10:30 a.m. and noon, draw so many worshippers from a radius of 30 to 40 miles that lines of people two or three deep customarily rim the walls, children crowd one another around the sanctuary and the overflow jams the choir loft. That is just as well – the choir does not need a loft anymore. The 30 voices are up front with the congregation, near the altar where they can lead the people in song or project their own music most advantageously.

What draws such standing-room-only attendance, while nearby parishes scramble to muster their faithful, is a joyous, meticulously planned and deliberately artistic liturgy.

These Masses in their five years have become something of a legend in church circles. The remarkable element is not so much the skill with which the various media, music included, are combined around a theme to project reverence and prayerfulness, but rather the response this programming has evoked. An unmistakable climate of worship pervades the Oakland Cathedral congregation. It appears, indeed, lifted up. To be there and share in celebrating mass is for many a spiritual experience.

Whether, this response is engendered by the choir, by a French horn or flute, by wall hangings, balloons or children's dialogue at the pulpit, by an outburst of applause at some particularly cheery upbeat music or by the open rapport between the priests at the altar and the people in the pews, or, more likely, by all elements combined, the masses are participatory celebrations.

Ecclesiastical visitors from throughout the world have been drawn to St. Francis de Sales. Among those who have voiced approval are Jesuit Father Juan Mateos, liturgical instructor at the Gregorian Institute in Rome, And Father C.J. McNaspy, also a Jesuit, who is an authority in religious music. Some liturgists have called the cathedral Mass the most creative parish expression of the Vatican II summons to community which has taken form anywhere in the world.

"When the time comes in Mass for the acclamation, and the people sing that powerful 'Amen' that you think will blow the walls out, that is the moment when you just feel the faith," said Monsignor Joseph H. Skillin, the Cathedral's youthful pastor. "The vibes get so thick you can cut them. As I see it, that's good. Joy is what the gospel is all about."

A combination of talents has made this service possible. Keystone, is Father Donald Osuna, a musician who has guided the liturgy development from the start, has meshed its eclectic scores "from Bach to rock," has written new music when none turned up to his taste, and has insisted upon professional standards to create an atmosphere fitting for prayer. It was Osuna whose remarks, quoted at the beginning of this story, defined the parish objective.

Osuna has been aided by an able choir director, John McDonnell, an attorney whose tough administrative rein has held the large choir and ensemble of six to eight professional musicians to a year-round schedule. The two men seem to complement each other.

MUSIC ISN'T ONLY MEDIUM

The impression is prevalent that what draws worshipers to the cathedral is the richness of its music. But that is only one medium used.

"In our society," McDonnell said, "we have a lot of tools available for communication which work better than a verbal sermon. We use everything we can to surround the administration of the sacraments with meaning – music, film, drama, dialogue, poetry, song, pageantry."

Sometimes a group of children can act out an idea more effectively than a priest can tell it. Sometimes a visitor serves best: a black minister or seminarians in a skit presenting a modern interpretation of the biblical prophets, or residents of Synanon, the rehabilitative drug center located within the parish, who composed an original cantata for a cathedral liturgy.

One memorable Sunday the sermon was delivered wordlessly – by a mime. Another time, slides showed a sequence of faces of migrant farm workers as the day's lesson. Balloons, costumes, stage effects, special lighting and film are used. The Black Catholic Caucus managed a triumphal mass last Christmas Eve, vibrant with the syncopation and passion of Negro music, concelebrated by all the black priests in the area, the readings and prayers built around repentance for racial discrimination.

For Mexican-Americans, converting Columbus Day into a salute for "La Raza" sent mariachi band music rocketing through the Gothic arches and sparked pride and self-importance in what had been the most self-effacing group in the parish. One summer series was devoted to "play," another to "humor." Summer school culminated once in a "Peanuts" mass, with the philosophy of the comic strip woven into the readings and youngsters costumed as Lucy or Charlie Brown.

McDonnell sees limits to experimentation. "We have a given situation – the administration of the Sacrament. There is only so much modification possible, for we stay strictly to a focus on the celebration. We are insistent about not losing the centrality of our worship and the sacrament."

But Osuna sees new possibilities. There has been change, year to year: a strengthening of talents, an expansion of media. This is no static formula. McDonnell and Osuna have scoffed at others to put their plans on paper for others to follow. Each liturgy, Osuna contends, must be a unique creation, the product of artists' endeavors for a specific congregation. The two men are wary of shocking the worshipers; with explanations and forewarnings, they bring them along.

A new venture is electronic music. Pursuing his education in music at Mills College, Osuna has composed a special quadraphonic "Vigil of Easter" electronic mass, which was premiered Holy Saturday. Osuna himself installed the four channels and console to deliver it, and these will be available permanently in the cathedral.

The ingredients in use at Oakland are not unique. Many parishes enrich the Mass with contemporary ballads, community singing, even rock and recitation. The Oakland Cathedral liturgy differs in the professional standards applied, the long range planning involved and the experience acquired by a group which has been together for seven years, overseeing a continually evolving liturgy. Musicians, all professional players or university-level musician students, are paid. Choir members are volunteers but they rehearse rigorously. Unlike many experimental masses, the ceremony is carefully structured there is no spur-of-the-moment improvisation.

One sad reality, as McDonnell sees it, is that the Catholic Church, especially in America has no recent artistic tradition in music. When liturgical changes came about, he laments, cities with vast music resources – opera, symphony, music schools, fresh, youthful artists – settled for repeating weekly the same four hymns, with maybe the same teenage guitar player.

"The lack of common sense in dealing with something fundamentally supposed to be a celebration is appalling," McDonnell said. "At the Oakland Cathedral we are trying to be musical about what we do."

Osuna concedes mistakes happen. "Sure we blow it every now and then. But when the music fizzles, that happiness and prayerfulness keep right on coming. We've learned it's not what we provide that matters. It's what the people bring. They've discovered a worshiping community can be open, friendly and joyful."

The ecclesiastical year is blocked out into a sequence of large themes appropriate to the religious season. Those themes are interpreted in each Sunday's program, and the music, readings and amplification are keyed into the message. Particular attention is paid to developing the sermon. So detailed is the preparation, programs are even printed, containing songs and prayers for each Sunday. This eliminates the distraction of a congregation leafing through hymnals. Nothing is neglected that can maximize the artistry of the celebration or diminish distractions to the worshipers.

'WE GET CRITICIZED FOR THEATRICALS'

Music is purposely eclectic. Osuna feels this fits the variety, heritage and experience represented in the congregation. For so polyglot a society as America, one-idiom masses (depending on organ only guitar only) are mistakes, he insists. Osuna and McDonnell mix old, familiar hymns with modern folk ballads, symphonic music with country, piano concertos with Negro Spirituals. They delight in the treasury of choral music reaching back to the Renaissance, largely untouched by Catholics.

"We get criticized for what people call theatricals," said McDonnell. (The word "production" does crop up often and McDonnell and Osuna are open about seeking artistic effects.) "But people come to pray together, not just to listen or look.

"The Mass in our culture is about the only contact people have with the Church," McDonnell points out. "We're trying to make that contact meaningful. We want to keep them coming back, so we do everything we can to make the celebration interesting, not boring."

But why such an emphasis on liturgy in a parish enveloped in social problems? St. Francis de Sales spans some of the sorriest urban areas in the region, peopled with the impoverished, the lonely, ill and unemployed; with men and women involved in crime and violence; with minorities sunk in hopelessness. Across the street from the Cathedral threshold is the Greyhound Bus depot; half a block off, a state half-way house for criminals; kitty-corner away, a main drag for alcoholics and drug users, a tawdry junk-street of raucous bars. Not far off, the Black Panther headquarters

When Skillin became pastor, he had a professional study made, using 1970 census reports, to get an accurate reading of the environment. He found: With 21,000- people living inside parish boundaries, a quarter - 5,000 – are single persons living alone; 23 percent are over 65 years. A few are wealthy and live in elegant apartments at one fringe of the parish; most live in public housing for the elderly, in a dollar-a-night flop houses, in modest retirement homes or rooming houses which ring downtown.

In race, 62 percent are white; 33 percent black. The geography of the parish is dominated by banks, department stores, and office buildings. It's a weekday milieu, solitary on Sundays. One of the most telling statistics: 88 percent of 12,000 dwelling units are occupied by renters and over half of these rented units are in structures with 10 or more units – an impersonal, isolated existence. In most of the area, rent runs less than $100 a month. Much of the property is below code standards. Health authorities found higher than usual mortality rates for children and adults, inadequate nutrition, high disease rates.

Such data can correct misapprehensions about parish characteristics or pinpoint logical social action. But the general problems were obvious five year ago when Monsignor Michael Lucid, who was pastor, his assistant, Father James T. Keeley, and Osuna pondered where to begin. Newly together and determined to work as a team, they felt overwhelmed. Lucid insisted on establishing priorities rather than slugging away at everything. Time, money and effort must be focused upon limited, fixed goals. The school existed; bettering it was an obvious priority. Today, with open, upgraded classrooms, individualized instruction and lavish use of teaching aides, the old brick hulk of a school is an oasis for ghetto children.

Searching for another handle to the community, the trio reasoned that rather than become one more activist social endeavor agency lost in the misery-maze, the church should do what church alone should do: Provide meaningful worship. Talent at hand, particularly Osuna, indicated that direction. Liturgy was the current fresh church interest.

TEACH NEW LITURGY TO PARISHIONERS

At the time Oakland's diocesan liturgical committee was already two years into educational venture. McDonnell and Osuna were among its leaders. They undertook 10-week visitations at a parish invitation, with a "task force" of choir, musicians, director, lectors, even ushers if necessary.

For six weeks they would school parishioners in the new liturgical approach to the celebration of the mass, training what music and talent was locally available. The last four Sundays they supervised production of the end- product. This venture seeded great interest in modern liturgy in the area. But by 1968 the task force was tired. Inviting it to make the cathedral its home base, to let is members' talents bloom into a liturgy model seemed logical.

One story is around that critics (many of them quite vociferous) besieged Bishop Floyd Begin of Oakland to shut the whole thing off, and that he agreed, if pastors lamenting the loss of their parishioners would guarantee the same people would attend as faithfully in their home parishes. The cathedral, as cathedral, is open to all, and keeps on drawing them, 1,000 to 1,500 twice each Sunday.

Much attention gets paid to outsiders. More than 60 percent of the two congregations are judged "visiting the parish." But overlooked is the attraction the liturgy had for the surrounding poor. The church draws an immense attendance of blacks, Mexican-Americans, Filipinos, Japanese and Chinese and other minorities from neighboring flatlands, by no means all Catholics. Even attendance at the traditional 7:30 and 9 o'clock Sunday Masses has tripled. The spark of the community when St. Francis de Sales' old people reach out a handclasp of peace to another during Mass seems almost sacramental. For many, it may be the only human contact of the week.

One offshoot is financial. Sunday collections, about $400 when the cathedral was in doldrums, now average $1,200. The school is prime beneficiary. Second to benefit are the elderly. Prompted by her own sense of mission, Sister Thomasine McMahon, a Holy Names Sister, three years ago volunteered to develop a parish program for the old folks. She is now chairman of the Oakland Committee on the Aging. It was clear the aged had to be a top parish priority.

Newest priority is community "outreach." A set of lay parish "task forces" has just undertaken to mesh the "Sunday parish" with the "weekday parish" on various projects. The cathedral is an inspiration to many parishes and a liturgy stimulant, but is too unique in structure and resources to be a valid model for most of the country. Many parishes may be further advanced in lay participation, social justice or even ecumenism, through rapport with its Protestant neighbors.

But it is not easy to mix people who have a geographical identity to this church, people whose resources are limited, with the effervescent young suburbanites who are drawn by the liturgy and its significance for their children, but who are ignorant (or innocent) of human problems in the neighborhood. These people pray beautifully together but they harbor suspicions about one another. Skillin expects the community of worship may generate a community of Christian concern especially as church.

WE WANT PEOPLE TO BE JOYFUL

"We won't force it. We will wait for it to happen," he said. "We just want people to be joyful and free, and do Christian things with their lives."

That a sense of community does exist, however, came clear when organizers for last January's conference on the Relevance of Organized Religion (the "In Search" Conference) selected St. Francis de Sales as one of its pivotal parishes for analysis. The cathedral won praise for the vitality of its liturgy, for the compassion of its service to the elderly and for its creative school. But more significant was the statement worked out by ordinary people from the parish. In a day's discussion, they defined, for the purposes of the conference-study, the essential value of the church's presence in their community. They said the liturgy "promotes the experience of Christian joy and active Christian concern for each other." The priests, listening on the periphery, were astonished. It wrapped up precisely what they aimed for.

Out of their dismal and deprived environment, the parishioners of the ghetto noted, with special emphasis, that St. Francis de Sale Cathedral is good because it "celebrates life."

Reprinted by permission of National Catholic Reporter
115 E. Armour Blvd, Kansas City, MO 64111   www.ncronline.org

Postlude
An Enculturated American "We"

By Jack Miffleton

I remember the first time I participated in an Oakland Cathedral liturgy. I was a student at the Jesuit School of Theology in Berkeley. I saw the Catholic Church as described by James Joyce in *Finnegan's Wake*: "Here comes everybody!" The diversity, the hospitality, the singing, the attention to liturgical symbolism, the attention to the spoken word! I was hooked! St. Francis de Sales became my spiritual home for the next decade. I soon found out that the paschal song of this community extended far beyond the liturgy into the world. Of course, I enjoy a bias, but the Cathedral experience was like a film of *Gaudium et Spes*, the Pastoral Constitution on the Church in the Modern World (Vatican Council II). Here I saw a church renewing itself with Christ clearly at the center.

In his reflections Don Osuna lets the reader see into the struggles of a young priest and artist in a time of great change and ambiguity in the Catholic Church. Students of church history and liturgy should read Don's memories of this transformative period. They will find a post-Vatican II community that took possession of its liturgy and let the liturgy possess them. During a period when new liturgical texts were being prepared, the Oakland Cathedral made transitional adaptations that should remind all liturgists that Divine Worship is not a product of its texts, but of a holy people. In his 2007 encyclical, *Spe Salvi* (*Saved in Hope*), Pope Benedict XVI refers to the "social reality" of salvation and how a redeemed life is "linked to a lived union with a people" and is only attained by the individual within the "We." The Oakland Cathedral experience is an example of such a "We," and more precisely an enculturated American "We."

CPSIA information can be obtained at www.ICGtesting.com
Printed in the USA
LVOW120636090112

262977LV00003B/4/P